Mighty Men
of Old

(From Jacob to the Dedication of Aaron)

VOLUME TWO

the Bible Story

Mighty Men of Old ❖ Volume Two

Arthur S. Maxwell
Author of Uncle Arthur's *Bedtime Stories*

When Arthur S. Maxwell wrote *The Bible Story*, he used the King James Version of the Bible, closely following its narrative. This edition continues that tradition and draws from other translations using language that today's children readily understand.

NEWLY REVISED AND ILLUSTRATED
More than 400 stories in 10 Volumes Covering the Entire Bible From Genesis to Revelation

REVIEW AND HERALD® PUBLISHING ASSOCIATION
HAGERSTOWN, MD 21740

This book was
Revised by Cheryl Holloway
Edited by Richard W. Coffen
Cover art by Harry Anderson

PRINTED IN U.S.A.

R&H Cataloging Service
Maxwell, Arthur Stanley,
1896-1970
      The Bible story.
      1. Bible stories.   I. Title.
II. Holloway, Cheryl Woolsey,
1956-
            220.9505

ISBN 0-8280-0796-9

When Jacob made
Joseph a beautiful coat
of many colors as a sign
of his affection, it
excited the envy of all
Joseph's brothers and
they began to plot how
they might destroy him.

PAINTING BY RUSSELL HARLAN

CONTENTS

PART ONE

Stories of

Jacob,
Esau, *and* Joseph

(Genesis 25:19-50:26)

So Much for So Little

(Genesis 25:19-34)

LIKE his father, Isaac had to wait a long time for a son of his own—60 years, in fact. Then he got two at once!

You can imagine the excitement of all the servants in the camp when twins were born to their master. Soon everybody was talking about the two little boys, Esau and Jacob. They especially liked the story of how Jacob, who was born last, grabbed his little brother's heel in his own tiny hand. They were sure this was a sign that he would become more important than his brother. Strangely, that is what happened.

To understand this story properly, you must remember that in those days the first boy to be born in a family became heir to twice as much of his father's property as his brothers would receive. Because Esau was born a few minutes before Jacob, this "birthright" belonged to him.

Even today in some countries, the same custom is followed. Most of what the father owns goes to the oldest son when the father dies.

9

While they were quite young boys, Esau and Jacob were different in character. Esau liked to hunt with his bow and arrow, but Jacob preferred to stay at home and tend the sheep.

While being the firstborn in any family meant a great deal, being Isaac's first-born meant much more. This child would inherit not only most of his father's possessions but also all the blessings that God had promised to Abraham. As a result, Esau was a very fortunate boy. Since he was lucky enough to be born first, two-thirds of Isaac's riches and honor would eventually be his.

Surprisingly, however, the birthright didn't mean a thing to him. He wasn't even interested. All he thought about was having a good time out in the fields and woods with his bow and arrows. He was more interested in being known as a skillful hunter and good shot rather than being the first-born son of Isaac.

Jacob was different. He didn't like hunting. He preferred to stay around the camp, where his mother told him stories about his father and grandfather and the promises God had made to them. He especially enjoyed the story about what happened at his birth when the Lord had told his mother, "The older will serve the younger." He didn't understand at first what this meant. But the more he thought about it, the more he wondered how he could get the birthright away from his brother.

Since he stayed home more than Esau, his mother grew to love him best. With one thing and another, the two boys gradually drifted apart.

This was sad, for surely twins should love each other in a special way all through life. How much better it would have been if they had played and worked together. Jacob could have shared the fun in the woods, and Esau could have stayed home a bit more to help around the camp and enjoy his mother's stories!

10

But it didn't work out that way. Soon both boys were treating each other like strangers.

One day Esau, feeling very hungry, came home from the fields. As he walked toward the tents, all he could think of was finding something to eat. And whom should he see getting the dinner ready but Jacob.

Mother's boy, doing the cooking now! he may have thought, but he didn't say it. He wanted food too badly.

"What do you have there?" he asked.

"Lentils," replied Jacob, continuing to stir the stew.

"Give me some," Esau said. "I'm famished."

But Jacob didn't care. Knowing that his brother was desperately hungry, he thought this might be his chance to get the birthright away from him. So he refused to give Esau any food unless Esau promised to trade with him.

"Trade?" Esau asked in surprise. "Trade what?"

"How about selling me the birthright for a nice, big bowl of lentils?"

"It's a deal," said Esau carelessly, grabbing for the bowl without even thinking about what his words meant for the future.

But Jacob didn't want Esau to be able to get out of the bargain. "Swear to me first," Jacob said.

"So he swore an oath to him, selling his birthright to Jacob. Then Jacob gave Esau some bread and some lentil stew. He ate and drank, and then got up and left. So Esau despised his birthright."

Afterward, of course, Esau realized what he had done and

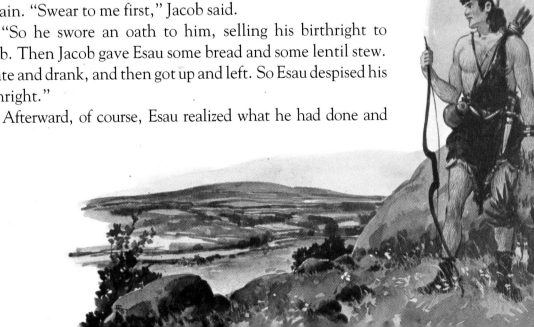

how much he had given away for one dish of lentils. He had given up most of his father's riches and the honor of being head of the house after his father's death. He had also given up the privilege of being the one through whom God's promises would be fulfilled—through whom Jesus, the Messiah, would come. All this had no more value to him than a few cents' worth of food.

So much for so little!

"Esau despised his birthright," the Bible says. He had treated something that was very important spiritually as if it meant nothing. Now "he could bring about no change of mind, though he sought the blessing with tears." [1]

He felt very sad about what he had done and begged Jacob to go back on the deal and leave things as they were before. But Jacob refused.

All of us—you, and I, and everybody—have to be careful not to make the same mistake. We also have a "birthright." We may be "heirs of God and co-heirs with Christ" [2] if we want to be. All the treasures of heaven will be ours if we are faithful to God. He has said that He will gladly let us live forever with Him, if only we will love Him and stay close to Him.

He has promised us so much! Let's make sure we never trade away these precious blessings for some little pleasure that will soon be gone. Our birthright is too rich a treasure to sell for a bowl of soup.

_____
[1] Hebrews 12:17.
[2] Romans 8:17.

Cheating Never Pays

(Genesis 27:1-45)

ESAU did not forgive his brother for cheating him out of his birthright. As for Jacob, he was not very happy about it either. He never felt quite sure that his father would honor the hard bargain he had made with his brother. All the time he was afraid that Isaac would ignore the deal as just a boyish prank and give the birthright to Esau anyway.

Year after year the twins drifted further and further apart. Esau spent more and more time hunting, and Jacob worked around the camp.

Meanwhile, Isaac was growing old—probably 137 years of age—and lost his sight. Thinking he was going to die, he sent for Esau. He wanted to give him a special parting blessing—just as though the birthright still belonged to him.

When Esau entered the tent, Isaac said to him, "My son. . . . I am now an old man and don't know the day of my death. Now then, get your weapons—your quiver and bow—and go out to the open country to hunt some wild game for me. Prepare me the kind of tasty food I like and bring it to me to eat, so that

13

I may give you my blessing before I die."

Esau was glad to do this favor for his father. He was even happier that the old man was not going to let Jacob get away with the birthright after all. So he hurried out, picked up his bow and arrows, and went off to hunt.

But, sad to say, Rebekah had been nearby and heard what Isaac had said about blessing Esau when he returned with the food. She wanted her favorite son, not Esau, to have the best of everything. So she quickly thought up a plan to get her own way.

Finding Jacob, Rebekah told him what had happened. She suggested that since Isaac was blind, it would be easy to fool him. "Listen carefully, and do just what I tell you," she said firmly. "Go out to the flock and bring me two choice young goats, so I can prepare some tasty food for your father, just the way he likes it. Then take it to your father to eat, . . . so that he may give you his blessing before he dies."

At first Jacob was slow to do it. He still wanted the blessing, but he was afraid that Isaac might find out who he really was.

"My brother Esau," he said, "is a hairy man, and I'm a man with smooth skin. What if my father touches me? I would appear to be tricking him and would bring down a curse on myself rather than a blessing."

Rebekah had set her heart on Jacob's getting that blessing, and she finally talked him into doing what she wanted. So

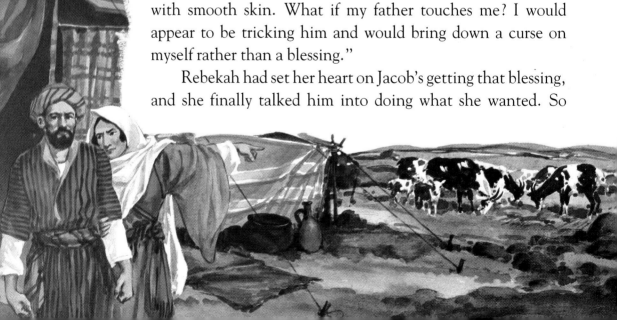

Jacob brought the two baby goats, and his mother cooked the kind of meal she knew Isaac loved.

Then she dressed Jacob in some of Esau's best clothes. In order to make sure Isaac was completely fooled, she put part of the skins of the kids on Jacob's hands and neck, where his father might touch him.

What a phony Jacob was when he went into his father's tent with that steaming plate of food! And how frightened he must have felt in case Isaac would discover his wicked trickery. It's a wonder he didn't spill the gravy all over the place. But he felt worse when Isaac began to act distrustful.

"Who is it?" asked the old man, trying hard to figure out just who had come into his tent.

"I am Esau your firstborn," Jacob said, trying to make his voice sound like Esau's. "I have done as you told me. Please sit up and eat some of my game so that you may give me your blessing."

Now Isaac became even more suspicious. "How did you find it so quickly, my son?" he asked.

"The Lord your God gave me success," said Jacob, making his crime worse by bringing God into it.

By this time Isaac was more sure than ever that something was wrong. "Come near so I can touch you, my son, to know whether you really are my son Esau or not."

Jacob, trembling with fear, moved toward his father.

Isaac began to touch him. He was puzzled. "The voice is

the voice of Jacob," he said, "but the hands are the hands of Esau."

He paused a moment, then said again, "Are you really my son Esau?"

And Jacob, lying to the last, replied, "I am."

Satisfied, Isaac ate the food Jacob had brought. Then he blessed him, saying, among other things, "May nations serve you. May peoples bow down to you. May you be master over your brothers. May your mother's sons bow down to you" (ICB).

Isaac had been thinking for days about all the good things he would promise Esau, his oldest son, who was so dear to him. Now he said them all to the wrong son!

Once Jacob received the blessing, he hurried out, tore off Esau's clothes, and tried to look as innocent as he could. But if he thought his brother would not find out, he was very wrong.

The Bible says, "After Isaac finished blessing him and Jacob had scarcely left his father's presence, his brother Esau came in from hunting."

Never dreaming that anything had gone wrong, Esau made the tasty meal and cheerfully carried it to his father. "My father, sit up," he said, "and eat some of my game, so that you may give me your blessing."

Then the blow fell.

← PAINTED AFTER DORÉ

With his mother's help Jacob put hairy skins over his arms and neck to deceive his blind father Isaac, so that he might receive the blessing intended for his older brother, Esau.

"Who are you?" demanded his father in a loud voice, angry that anyone should tease him like this.

Esau stood still, astonished. Didn't his father recognize him?

"I am your son, your firstborn, Esau."

"Who?" cried Isaac. He "trembled violently and said, 'Who was it, then, that hunted game and brought it to me? I ate it just before you came and I blessed him.' "

Esau was heartbroken. What he had thought might be his last labor of love for his dear old father had been completely spoiled. The food he had so carefully prepared with his own hands was not wanted. And now the blessing that Isaac had promised him had been given to someone else. It was too much. He broke down and wept, crying out "Bless me—me too, my father!"

Such a pitiful cry. But what could Isaac do? He had given the blessing to Jacob, and according to the custom of those days, he could not take it back.

18

He gave Esau another blessing, but it was not the same, and Esau knew it.

"Esau held a grudge against Jacob because of the blessing his father had given him. He said to himself, 'The days of mourning for my father are near; then I will kill my brother Jacob.' "

He not only said it to himself, he told his friends, and someone passed it on to Rebekah, and she told Jacob.

Jacob had been afraid that this might happen. Now he was really frightened. Rebekah decided that the only way he could save his life was to leave home at once. She suggested that he run away to his Uncle Laban's home in Haran.

"Stay with him for a while," she said, "until your brother's fury subsides. When your brother is no longer angry with you and forgets what you did to him, I'll send word for you to come back from there. Why should I lose both of you in one day?"

What a price Rebekah paid for this miserable deed! In one day she lost both her boys—and it broke her heart. Esau now hated her, and after Jacob left home, she never saw him again.

As for Jacob, he lost both his home and his mother. For years he was lonely, disappointed for what he had done, and always afraid Esau would catch up with him.

Some boys and girls today think that cheating is smart. It isn't. If you are ever tempted to deceive someone, think about Jacob and what it cost him for being so mean and deceitful. Cheating never pays.

The Stairway From Earth to Heaven

(Genesis 27:46; 28:1-22)

THAT last night Jacob spent at home must have been anything but happy. Esau was furious. Jacob was afraid. Everybody in the camp guessed that something terrible had happened.

Rebekah went to see Isaac and tried to smooth over what Jacob had done. Then she changed the subject. "Jacob needs to get married," she said and went on to tell Isaac how worried she was that he would choose one of the daughters of Heth. "If Jacob takes a wife from among the women of this land, from Hittite women like these, my life will not be worth living."

Isaac agreed that Jacob should go to his mother's relatives in Haran and find a wife among the daughters of his uncle Laban. Now, at least, Rebekah didn't have to tell people the real reason why Jacob left home so suddenly.

Isaac called for Jacob and told him what he was to do. So Jacob "obeyed his father and mother"—even though he was 77 years old—and headed for Haran.

It was a sad goodbye. Think of his mother's tears, his

father's worry, his own heartbreak. Perhaps they guessed they would never see each other again. What a price to pay for doing wrong!

Sick with worry and loneliness, Jacob trudged along on the trail that led to Haran. No camels for him like Eliezer had taken when he went to find a wife for Isaac. He was in disgrace, and he knew it. The more he thought about what he had done, the more he despised himself. What a fool he had been! How much he had lost, and how little he had gained! He might be heir to his father's riches, but here he was, alone and penniless, running for his life from his own twin brother.

When evening came, Jacob, tired and homesick, flung himself on the ground. Maybe sleep would help him forget his troubles. He didn't have any of the comforts he had enjoyed at home now. "Taking one of the stones there, he put it under his head and lay down to sleep" on the hard ground.

Never had he felt so low, so wretched, so far from God, as at that moment. But God was very near.

As Jacob slept, "He had a dream in which he saw a stairway resting on the earth, with its top reaching to heaven, and the angels of God were ascending and descending on it.

"There above it stood the Lord, and he said: 'I am the Lord, the God of your father Abraham and the God of Isaac. I will give you and your descendants the land on which you are lying. Your descendants will be like the dust of the earth, and you will spread out to the west and to the east, to the north and to the south. All peoples on earth will be blessed through you and your

offspring. I am with you and will watch over you wherever you go, and I will bring you back to this land. I will not leave you until I have done what I have promised you.'

"When Jacob awoke from his sleep, he thought, 'Surely the Lord is in this place, and I was not aware of it.' "

How could God have talked like this to such a mean, low-down fellow? Didn't He know how bad Jacob had been? Yes, God knew everything about him. But the most wonderful thing about God is that He is always willing to forgive even the worst sinners. To the meanest and the most selfish, to all the Jacobs in the world, He says, "Come now, let us reason together. . . . Though your sins are like scarlet, they shall be as white as snow; though they are red as crimson, they shall be like wool." [1]

This was what God was trying to say to Jacob that night as he slept with his head on a rock, "Look up! There's a way back. There's a stairway from earth to heaven, and you can climb it."

When Jacob woke up and thought about his dream, his heart was touched. He cried out with tears in his eyes, "This is the gate of heaven." The place must have seemed like the entrance into heaven, as he thought of the

MARCUS MASHBURN

wonderful shining stairway stretching up into the sky, with the angels moving up and down on it and the glory of the Lord above it.

As Jacob thought of God's kindness and how tenderly He had spoken, he made up his mind that from that moment on he would live a better life. He made God a promise, saying, "If God will be with me and will watch over me on this journey I am taking and will give me food to eat and clothes to wear so that I return safely to my father's house, then the Lord will be my God. . . . And of all that you give me I will give you a tenth."

It was the prayer of a worried, hungry, home-sick man taking his first halting step toward heaven, but God was glad for it and accepted it. He also rejoices when any of us comes back to Him, no matter what words we use to tell Him we are sorry for our sins.

That stairway from earth to heaven was God's way of telling us all that no matter how bad we may have been, we may come back to Him anytime we want to. He has a stairway leading from wherever we are right up to the throne of glory!

Is that stairway really there? It certainly is, and you may climb it whenever you want to. The stairway is Jesus, who once said to His disciple Nathanael, "You shall see heaven open, and the angels of God ascending and descending upon the Son of Man." [2]

Yes, Jesus is "the way, and the truth, and the life. No one comes to the Father" but by Him. [3]

When we know we have done wrong and we feel just as low as Jacob did when he was lying on the hard ground, we can think of that beautiful stairway. We can see it going straight up from our tear-stained pillow into heaven. Above it we can see the glory of God and know that He is waiting to forgive us, waiting to say, "I am with you and will watch over you wherever you go," and "I will not leave you."

Did you do something wrong today? Were you cross, unkind, nasty, deceitful? Are you sorry? Do you want to be good? The stairway is beside you. Use it. Climb back to God right now!

---

[1] Isaiah 1:18.
[2] John 1:51.
[3] John 14:6.

A Long, Long Lesson

(*Genesis 29; 30:25-34; 31; 32:1, 2*)

AFTER many long, hot days of walking and many sad and lonely nights lying on the hard ground, Jacob's journey was nearly over.

He was now in his mother's country—the land she had told him about so many times when he was a child. Now he was seeing it for the first time.

One morning as he trudged along in the warm sunshine, "he saw a well in the field, with three flocks of sheep lying near it. . . . The stone over the mouth of the well was large."

Glad to have someone to talk to after being alone so long, Jacob went over to the shepherds and spoke to them.

"Where are you from?" he asked.

"We're from Haran," they replied.

"Do you know Laban, Nahor's grandson?" asked Jacob.

"Yes, we know him," they answered.

"Is he well?"

"Yes, he is," replied the shepherds, "and here comes his daughter Rachel with the sheep."

25

Eagerly Jacob looked at the beautiful girl approaching the well with a flock of her father's sheep. He forgot that it was noon and that nobody was supposed to open the well until evening. He rolled away the heavy stone and began to draw water for Rachel's sheep.

Never had a humble task like this seemed so pleasant to him. It didn't seem to take any time at all, not with this lovely girl smiling at him. She was so much like his mother!

When he finished drawing the water, he ran over to Rachel, kissed her, and burst into tears! He explained that he was her Aunt Rebekah's son, and she was so excited that she ran home at once and told her father. Laban came hurrying out, and when he saw Jacob "he embraced him and kissed him and brought him to his home."

Jacob spent a very happy month in Laban's household, and when his uncle suggested he stay longer and work for him, Jacob

said he would. Then Laban asked him what wages he would expect.

"Just Rachel," he said. He wanted no other reward, he loved her so much. "I'll work for you seven years in return for your younger daughter Rachel."

Laban agreed, and "Jacob served seven years to get Rachel, but they seemed like only a few days to him because of his love for her."

Jacob worked very hard for his uncle. As he said later, "the heat consumed me in the daytime and the cold at night, and sleep fled from my eyes." But problems like these didn't matter. He felt he could endure anything just so he could have Rachel for his wife.

The seven years came to an end. Everything seemed to be going well. The wedding day was fixed, and Laban arranged for the feast.

Then Jacob suffered the biggest disappointment any man could have. By a sly trick, Laban gave his oldest daughter Leah to Jacob in marriage, instead of Rachel. This was just as wrong and mean as the time Jacob had misled his father by pretending he was Esau.

You can imagine how angry Jacob was when he discovered he had been deceived. "What is this you have done to me?" he cried. "I served you for Rachel, didn't I? Why have you deceived me?"

Poor Jacob! He was learning something he needed to know—what it feels like to be cheated. By a long, long lesson he was being taught that it never pays to lie and deceive.

Now we see Laban's character a little more clearly. He was a hard bargainer if ever there was one. Yes, he told Jacob, he would keep his word to let him have Rachel, but that would require seven more years of service.

Seven more years! It didn't seem fair, but Jacob agreed to his uncle's terms. What else could he do?

When the second seven years were up, Jacob decided to leave and return to his old home in Canaan. He'd had enough.

"Give me my wives and children," he said, "and let me go."

But Laban knew when he was well off so begged him to stay. "The Lord has blessed me because of you."

Once more Jacob agreed to stay, this time for wages, but the next six years were not happy. True, he now had flocks and

28

herds of his own, which seemed to multiply more rapidly than Laban's, but Laban kept changing Jacob's wages. Then, too, Laban's sons became more and more jealous of Jacob. They thought that he was getting rich at their expense.

So Jacob talked it over with Rachel and Leah. They agreed that it would be better for everybody if they just packed up and left, even if they had to go without telling their father, Laban.

Then one night the Lord appeared to Jacob and said, "I am the God of Bethel, where you anointed a pillar and where you made a vow to me. Now leave this land at once and go back to your native land."

This touched Jacob's heart, for Bethel was the place where, 20 years earlier, he had seen the stairway reaching from earth to heaven. How wonderful, he thought, that God still remembered the vow he made that night to live a better life! Now Jacob was quite sure he should leave Laban and return to his old home.

"Jacob put his children and his wives on camels, and he drove all his livestock ahead of him, along with all the goods he had accumulated, . . . to go to his father Isaac in the land of Canaan."

"Moreover, Jacob deceived Laban the Aramean by not

telling him he was running away." Hurrying as fast as possible, he ferried his family and his property over the River Euphrates and made for Mount Gilead on the border of Canaan.

Jacob got a good start on his uncle. Laban didn't learn until three days later what had happened. Now it was Laban's turn to feel tricked, and he didn't like it. Gathering a band of men, he hurried after Jacob, determined to bring him back.

On the way, God spoke to Laban in a dream. "Be careful not to say anything to Jacob, either good or bad." God knew that Laban would probably begin with pleasant words and end up with angry ones like so many people do. He didn't want Laban to try to bribe or threaten Jacob, in order to make him come back.

Meanwhile, Jacob hurried on as fast as he could, but with such a large family and so many cattle, it was impossible to keep ahead. Finally, after a seven days' chase, Laban caught up with him at Mount Gilead.

"What have you done?" cried Laban, as he came puffing up to Jacob. "Why did you run off secretly and deceive me? Why didn't you tell me, so I could send you away with joy and singing to the music of tambourines and harps? You didn't even let me kiss my grandchildren and my daughters goodbye."

Jacob knew that Laban had never intended to let him go, and that all this about making a farewell feast for him was just so much talk. He gave Laban a piece of his mind, reminding him of all his long and faithful service.

Then he said, "It was like this for the twenty years I was in your household. I worked for you fourteen years for your two daughters and six years for your flocks, and you changed my wages ten times. If the God of my father, the God of Abraham and the Fear of Isaac, had not been with me, you would surely have sent me away empty-handed. But God has seen my hardship and the toil of my hands, and last night he rebuked you."

Laban began to cool off. He could tell that Jacob was determined to go back to Canaan and that he could do nothing about it. He suggested that they make peace. Jacob agreed.

Following a custom of those days, they all began piling up stones to form a memorial. Laban called it " Jegar Sahadutha." It was also called "Mizpah," meaning "a beacon, or watchtower." He said, "May the Lord keep watch between you and me when we are away from each other." It was a happy ending to what might have been a very serious quarrel.

Early the next morning they told each other goodbye. "Laban kissed his grandchildren and his daughters and blessed them" and went back home.

Struggle in the Night

(Genesis 32:1-13, 23-33)

JACOB'S long, long lesson was not over yet. He had much more to learn before he could become the truly great man God wanted him to be.

No sooner was he out of one trouble than he was in another. As he waved goodbye to his uncle Laban he began to worry about Esau and what would happen if they met again.

That night, as he went on his way, "the angels of God met him." This cheered his heart, for they reminded him of the angels he had seen on the stairway up to heaven, but the next day he was worrying again.

Finally he decided to send messengers to Esau to find out if he was still angry after 20 years had passed. When the messengers returned a few days later, their report troubled Jacob. Had Esau not changed his mind at all? "We went to your brother Esau," said the messengers, "and now he is coming to meet you, and four hundred men are with him."

Four hundred men! What could Jacob do against so many?

STRUGGLE IN THE NIGHT

No wonder he was "in great fear and distress." All he could think of doing was to divide his caravan into two parts so that if Esau attacked one group, the other might possibly escape. It wasn't much of a way out, and he knew it.

In his anxiety he turned to God. "O God of my father Abraham," he cried, "God of my father Isaac, O Lord, who said to me, 'Go back to your country and your relatives, and I will make you prosper,' I am unworthy of all the kindness and faithfulness you have shown your servant. I had only my staff when I crossed this Jordan, but now I have become two groups.

"Save me, I pray, from the hand of my brother Esau. . . . But you have said, 'I will surely make you prosper and will make your descendants like the sand of the sea, which cannot be counted.' "

Jacob's prayer shows how much closer to God he had grown during his long, hard years with Laban. Now he was grateful for all that God had done for him and given him. Most important of all, he was humble at last and willing to admit that he didn't deserve even the smallest of God's gifts.

That night Jacob sent his family over the brook Jabbok to what seemed the safest place in sight. He didn't go with them, for he wanted to be alone. He needed to talk with God all by himself. In the dark silence he flung himself on his knees, confessed his sins, and asked again for help.

Suddenly Jacob felt himself gripped by strong hands. He

started up in terror. Perhaps one of Esau's men had found him, or possibly some roving robber had crept up on him. He struggled to get free, but it was not easy. He wrestled on until daybreak, and then the Stranger touched Jacob's hip. His hip socket went out of joint, and Jacob was in great pain.

Suddenly Jacob realized that the Man he was fighting with was not a common thief or one of Esau's men. It was the Lord Himself. Like so many of us today, he had been in the arms of God and had not realized it.

Now, instead of trying to break away, Jacob held on. "I will not let you go unless you bless me," he cried.

The Lord said, "What is your name?"

"Jacob," he said meekly. His name meant "supplanter" or cheat.

"Your name will no longer be Jacob, but Israel, because you have struggled with God and with men and have overcome." The name Israel means "may God strive" or "he who struggles with God."

Jacob called the place "Peniel," meaning "the face of God." Because, he said, "I saw God face to face, and yet my life was spared."

A new day had dawned for Jacob. He had passed the great turning point of his life. He had found God for himself at last. His fears were gone. Courage and hope filled his heart. He was a new man. The coward, the cheat, the swindler, had become a prince of God.

It was like walking out of darkness into sunshine.

35

◄ PAINTING BY HARRY ANDERSON

In the early morning Jacob found himself wrestling with an angel of God, whose power he could not overcome. Tired and lame, Jacob then pleaded with the angel for his blessing.

The Twins Make Peace

(Genesis 32:13-21; 33:1-16)

NOW THAT Jacob had made peace with God, he wanted to make peace with his brother.

He had told God he was sorry for his sins, and now he was ready to tell Esau the same thing. There was no pride in his heart anymore or any desire to cheat or deceive. He was now a "prince of God" and wanted to do right.

The day before, he had sent a present to Esau as a token of his love. He had sent "two hundred female goats and twenty male goats, two hundred ewes and twenty rams, thirty female camels with their young, forty cows and ten bulls, and twenty female donkeys and ten male donkeys." It would be an expensive gift today, and it surely was then.

Jacob had sent the animals group by group, telling the servants in charge of each to say when they met Esau, "They belong to your servant Jacob. They are a gift sent to my lord Esau, and he is coming behind us."

Jacob's idea was to impress Esau with the greatness of his gift as he met one group after another. "I will pacify him with these gifts I am sending on ahead;" he said, "later, when I see him, perhaps he will receive me."

Just in case the present, big as it was, might not be enough to soften Esau's heart, Jacob arranged for the women and children to follow next. In front he put Leah's and Rachel's maids with their children, then Leah with her six little boys, and Dinah, her daughter. Dear Rachel with her precious Joseph came last.

As the caravan moved slowly onward in its new order, someone up ahead raised the cry, "Esau is coming!" The word was passed back from one to another, leaving everybody very afraid. Everybody, that is, except Jacob. He wasn't afraid anymore.

Brave in the new strength he had received from God, Jacob walked boldly forward, past his wives and children. He "bowed down to the ground seven times" as he came nearer and nearer to his brother. He couldn't think of anything more to show that he was truly sorry for what

he had done and that he wanted to be friends again.

Esau's heart melted at sight of his brother kneeling before him. "Esau ran to meet Jacob and embraced him; he threw his arms around his neck and kissed him. And they wept."

What a lovely meeting! How happy it must have made all the women and children, and all Esau's men too! I wouldn't be surprised if a lot of those people were wiping their eyes as the long-separated twins met and made peace.

Esau asked about all the women and children in Jacob's party, and one by one they came up and were introduced.

Then he asked, "What do you mean by all these droves I met?"

"To find favor in your eyes, my lord," said Jacob, smiling through his tears.

"I already have plenty, my brother," said Esau, thanking him. "Keep what you have for yourself."

Jacob pressed him to accept the present, and Esau finally agreed to do so.

Esau then showed his care and warmth by offering to go ahead of Jacob's caravan with his 400 men, as a bodyguard for the rest of the journey.

Jacob thanked him but said Esau didn't need to. Anyway, the bodyguard might want to travel too quickly.

"My lord knows that the children are tender," he said, "and that I must care for the ewes and cows that are nursing their young. If they are driven hard just one day, all the animals will die. . . . I move along slowly at the pace of the droves before me and that of the children."

Esau saw the wisdom of this, but he was so eager to do something for his brother that he offered to leave his men with Jacob to help with the work.

Again Jacob thanked him but said it wasn't necessary. He would be all right.

Then, with many smiles and kisses and handshakes, the brothers left each other again. They parted in peace, with everything forgiven.

As Esau and his men rode away I expect they kept turning around to wave goodbye. Jacob waved too, and so did Leah and Rachel. And how the children waved their little hands over and over again!

It was such a happy farewell this time, so different from that other one 20 years before.

Sold Into Slavery

(Genesis 33:17-20; 35; 37:1-28)

MOVING slowly along, Jacob and his caravan came at last to a place called Shechem. Everybody was tired of traveling, and the place looked rather nice, so he decided to settle there. He bought a piece of land just outside the city for 100 pieces of silver and set up camp.

But it didn't work out well. Some of his children got into serious trouble with the children of the city, and God told Jacob to move to Bethel.

"Settle there," the Lord said to him; "and build an altar there to God, who appeared to you when you were fleeing from your brother Esau."

They all needed to remember God. Things had been slipping. Some of Jacob's servants had been getting interested in the idols that the people of the land worshiped. The girls were dressing themselves up with ornaments, just like the heathen. They all needed to get back to Bethel, to "the house of God" and "the gate of heaven."

"So Jacob said to his household and to all who were with

40

him, 'Get rid of the foreign gods you have with you, and purify yourselves and change your clothes.' . . . So they gave Jacob all the foreign gods they had and the rings in their ears."

When Jacob later moved from Bethel, something very sad happened. Rachel died, just as she was having her second baby. Jacob was heartbroken, for he loved Rachel best of all.

As she was dying, Rachel named her baby Benoni, meaning "son of my sorrow." Jacob changed it to Benjamin, meaning "son of the right hand," which showed how much he thought of him. From now on, Rachel's two boys, Joseph and Benjamin, became especially precious to their sorrowing father.

Jacob now had 12 sons, and you really should know all their names: Reuben, Simeon, Levi, Judah, Issachar, Zebulun, Joseph, Benjamin, Dan, Naphtali, Gad, Asher.

Besides all these boys, there was Dinah and possibly other daughters whose names we do not know. Altogether it was a very large family. No wonder Jacob needed such huge flocks and herds to feed them all!

All the boys helped with the farm chores, spending much of their time taking care of the sheep and looking after all their father's animals. They were shepherds, cowboys, and farmers all in one. I imagine they were quite a husky group of boys.

But somehow Joseph didn't fit in with his older brothers. They looked at him as "little brother" and a bit of a nuisance. Once he told his father some of the bad things they were saying and doing, and they found out about it. After that, they didn't

41

like to have him around at all. They didn't want him telling on them again.

Because Joseph was Rachel's son, Jacob favored him more than the others, which helped make things worse. One day Jacob made a beautiful robe for Joseph. It was richly ornamented and very colorful. It made him stand out from the rest of his brothers.

This made the older brothers more jealous of him than ever. They said their father had never given them robes as good as that. They began to suspect that Jacob might be planning to give the birthright to Joseph instead of to Reuben.

When Joseph was 17 years old, he told his brothers about a dream he had had. He said they were all tying sheaves of grain in a field when suddenly all their sheaves bowed down to his sheaf. You can imagine how his brothers liked that!

Then he told them of another dream—how the sun, moon, and 11 stars bowed down to him. They liked that dream even less.

Joseph would have been wiser to have kept these dreams to himself or to have shared them only with his father. But the fact that he told them to his brothers may show how innocent he really was. Perhaps he hoped they would tell him what the dreams meant.

As it was, he succeeded in making the older boys very angry. They had no intention of bowing down to their little brother. They became so angry with him that they even talked about killing him.

One day his brothers saw him walking toward them across the fields. " 'Here comes that dreamer!' they said to each other. 'Come now, let's kill him and throw him into one of these cisterns and say that a ferocious animal devoured him. Then we'll see what comes of his dreams.' "

Just then Reuben walked up and overheard what the others were suggesting. Although he disliked Joseph as much as the rest, he wasn't willing to go so far as to kill him. Since he was the oldest, he knew his father would hold him responsible.

43

" 'Let's not take his life,' he said. 'Don't shed any blood. Throw him into this cistern here in the desert, but don't lay a hand on him.' " He planned to pull Joseph out later and send him back home.

The others agreed and waited for their brother to arrive.

Joseph had walked a long, long way—about 50 miles (80 kilometers)—looking for his brothers and was feeling very happy that he had found them at last. He was so glad to see them again that he almost forgot how tired and hungry he was.

Imagine, then, his disappointment when he saw the hateful looks on their faces. This was not the welcome he had expected. Suddenly, to his horror, some of them seized him, tore off his robe, carried him to a deep pit, and threw him in.

Joseph begged them to have mercy on him, but they wouldn't listen. They just left him alone at the bottom of the pit—hungry, cold, and heartbroken. He called and called, but no one came. For all he knew, they had left him to die of thirst and starvation.

Meanwhile, Reuben had gone back to his work. The others, left to themselves, started to talk about what to do with Joseph. They were in trouble. Since they had agreed not to kill the boy, they couldn't leave him in the pit to die. But if they let him go, he would run home and tell his father how cruel they had been to him.

Just then they saw a caravan approaching and discovered that it was a group of Ishmaelites from Gilead. "Their camels were loaded with spices, balm and myrrh, and they were on their way to take them down to Egypt."

Judah had a bright idea. "Come," he said, "let's sell him to the Ishmaelites."

The very thing! The brothers liked the idea because they would not only get rid of Joseph but would also be making some money as well.

So they stopped the caravan, and the bargaining began. Finally Joseph was lifted out of the pit. In spite of his tears

45

and pleading, his own brothers sold him to the Ishmaelites for 20 pieces of silver. Poor Joseph, the pride and joy of his father's heart, became a slave in a caravan on its way to Egypt.

How cruel family members can be sometimes! I hope you never have any thoughts like these about your little brother or sister.

Looking back, we can see what a wicked, foolish thing those brothers did. Selling Joseph didn't help them at all. The 20 pieces of silver didn't go far among 10 brothers—just two pieces each, which didn't take long to spend.

And they never really got rid of Joseph. For years after he was gone they couldn't get him out of their minds. They worried about what they had done and what might happen to them if they were ever found out. Why, possibly they might even meet Joseph again someday. And those dreams of his—what did they mean?

Could it be that they had made a dreadful mistake? They certainly had.

A Sad, Sad Journey

(Genesis 37:29-35)

THE ISHMAELITES' caravan had just disappeared into the twilight when Reuben returned to the pit to set Joseph free. Imagine how shocked he was to discover that the boy was no longer there!

Finding his brothers, he said in alarm, "The boy isn't there! Where can I turn now?"

He couldn't bear the thought of facing his father without Joseph. It would break the old man's heart. And he simply couldn't tell him that they had all been mean and cruel enough to sell him as a slave!

Then someone suggested a way out. They would tell Jacob a lie—that Joseph had been killed by some wild animal. To make the story seem true, they took Joseph's special robe and dipped it in the blood of a goat and carried it to Jacob.

"We found this," they said. "Examine it to see if it is your son's robe."

Jacob knew it, of course. "It is my son's robe!" he said with a sob. "Some ferocious animal has devoured him. Joseph has

surely been torn to pieces."

So Jacob, who had deceived his father, was now deceived by his own sons.

"Then Jacob . . . mourned for his son many days. All his sons and daughters came to comfort him, but he refused to be comforted. 'No,' he said, 'in mourning will I go down to the grave to my son.' So his father wept for him."

How those brothers could have tried to comfort their poor old father without once telling him the truth is more than I can imagine. But they didn't dare tell what they had done. If they had, who could say what their father might do in his terrible anger?

Meanwhile poor Joseph, sad, weary, and homesick, was on his way to Egypt. Just think. Only 17, and sold as a slave!

As Joseph trudged along the dusty trail with his Ishmaelite masters, many tears must have run down his cheeks. Why, oh, why, had all this evil come upon him? he wondered. Why had his brothers been so cruel to him? Why had they let him be taken away by strangers like this? Why hadn't anybody come to his rescue?

As it grew dark on that first night away from home, he must have felt terribly lonely. He couldn't help thinking about his comfortable bed at home, his pets, and all the things a boy cares for most. Then he must have thought of his father . . . and his little brother Benjamin . . . and his mother, who had died. That made him cry again.

What a sad, sad journey it was! The nearer the caravan came to Egypt, the farther it got from home. Joseph must have

← PAINTING BY HARRY ANDERSON

Joseph had never been away from home, but now he was sold by his cruel brothers as a slave to rough strangers, who took him far away from home over a hot, dusty road to Egypt.

wondered if he would ever see his home again. Many times he must have worried about what would happen to him in the foreign land to which the Ishmaelites were taking him. He knew he would soon be sold again, but to whom? It might be to somebody very harsh and cruel, who would make his life miserable.

Then he thought about God, his father's God. Though the Bible doesn't say so, we may be sure he prayed many times that God would look after him and somehow help him find his loved ones again someday.

And also we may be sure God was watching over this dear boy, just as He watches over every boy and girl who loves and trusts Him.

God knew that this sad journey into slavery was the best thing that could have happened to Joseph. Though Joseph did not understand it then, God was using his brothers' unkindness to lead him to a great future that otherwise he would never have known.

God often does that. He brings great blessing and happiness out of something that for a while seems very hard to bear. He loves to lead His trusting children out of darkness into light.

At last Joseph arrived in Egypt. He gazed wide-eyed at its great cities, its huge temples, its mighty pyramids, its mysterious Sphinx, and all the throngs of strange-looking people. He never dreamed for a moment that someday he would be a ruler in this country.

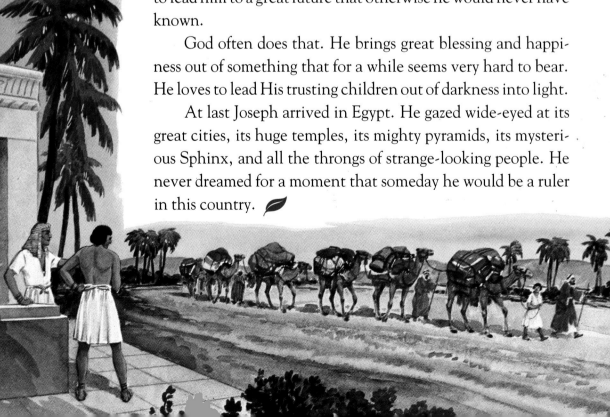

Two Strange Dreams

(Genesis 37:36; 39; 40)

EAGER to get rid of Joseph at a profit, the Ishmaelites sold him to Potiphar, captain of the guard in Pharaoh's court. He wanted a boy to help around his house. And so the son of one of the richest men in Canaan, who but a few days before had enjoyed everything he wanted in his father's house, was now no more than a slave at the beck and call of a heathen master.

It must have been very hard for poor Joseph to take, but he made up his mind that with God's help he would make the best of it. Whatever he was asked to do, he did well and faithfully.

Everybody around liked his pleasant manners. He was a great favorite with Potiphar himself, who gradually gave Joseph more and more important tasks to do. The Bible says, "His master saw that the Lord was with him and that the Lord gave him success in everything he did."

Not a word reached him from his old home. Nobody came to set him free. He was on his own, alone in the world. As the days and weeks and years went by, he tried hard to live a good,

clean, upright life. His honesty, truthfulness, and gracious spirit made a great impression on Potiphar. Joseph was a faithful witness for God and for the truths he had been taught in boyhood by his father and mother.

One day Potiphar told Joseph that from now on he would be "in charge of his household"—business manager of all his affairs. This was quite a promotion for a slave, and Joseph must have been very happy about it. No doubt he decided to try still harder to please his master.

Soon his wisdom and his winning ways were making everything run with wonderful smoothness in Potiphar's household. "The Lord blessed the household of the Egyptian because of Joseph. The blessing of the Lord was on everything Potiphar had, both in the house and in the field."

Potiphar was so pleased with Joseph that "he left in Joseph's care everything he had; with Joseph in charge, he did not concern himself with anything except the food he ate."

Then, just as everything was going so well, a terrible thing happened. Potiphar's wife falsely accused Joseph of doing some-

52

thing very wrong. Her story was untrue and terribly unfair, but her husband felt that he could do nothing else but throw Joseph into prison.

It was enough to break Joseph's heart. He knew he was innocent. He had taken a firm stand for the right. When enticed to do evil, he had nobly said, "How . . . could I do such a wicked thing and sin against God?" And now here he was in prison, chained in a dungeon like a common criminal! All his faithful witness for God seemed to have been worth nothing.

It is hard to be blamed for something you didn't do, isn't it? But Joseph would not let himself lose hope. Night after night as he lay in his cell, the iron shackles hurting his ankles, he remembered the story that Jacob, his father, had told him. Jacob had described how he had struggled in the night and how he held on to God until the sun came up. And Joseph made up his mind that he too would be a prince of God and hold on.

Because of his decision to be faithful to the Lord whatever happened, "the Lord was with him; he showed him kindness and granted him favor in the eyes of the prison warden."

What a fine young man he must have been to have made the same good impression on everybody, no matter where he was. Even in prison!

He was a born leader, and pretty soon the prison warden placed him in charge of all the other prisoners. He trusted Joseph so completely that he "paid no attention to anything under Joseph's care, because the Lord was with Joseph and gave him success in whatever he did."

One day two new prisoners arrived. One was Pharaoh's chief cupbearer, and the other was his chief baker. Just what they had done wrong we are not told. Probably it had something to do with the food and drink they had given his majesty. Whatever it was, it had made Pharaoh angry, and he had ordered them to be put in prison.

Joseph was able to sympathize with them, for he knew what it was like to be unfairly punished. He was friendly to them, and they liked him for it.

One morning when he went to see them in their cell, he noticed they were both looking very worried.

"Why do you look so sad today?" he asked cheerfully. "Anything wrong?"

Then they told him how they had both dreamed strange dreams and couldn't understand their meaning.

"Do not interpretations belong to God?" said Joseph. "Tell

me your dreams." He let them know that he was a servant of the God of heaven, the God who knows everything and who is willing to help His faithful children whenever they need Him.

So the chief cupbearer told Joseph his dream. It was about a vine that had three branches. On the branches buds appeared, which opened into blossoms. The blossoms became clusters of grapes, which ripened. Finally the cupbearer picked the grapes, squeezed them into Pharaoh's cup, and put the cup in his hand.

It was a very simple dream, but the cupbearer was sure it had some important meaning.

"You are right. It does," said Joseph. "The three branches are three days. Within three days Pharaoh will lift up your head and restore you to your position, and you will put Pharaoh's cup in his hand, just as you used to do when you were his cupbearer."

You can imagine how pleased the chief cupbearer was when he got this good news. His sadness vanished, and he felt very thankful to Joseph for interpreting his dream like this.

Joseph saw a chance to get himself out of prison. " 'When all goes well with you,' he said to the chief cupbearer, 'remember me and show me kindness; mention me to Pharaoh and get me out of this prison. For I was forcibly carried off from the land of the Hebrews, and even here I have done nothing to deserve being put in a dungeon.' "

The cupbearer gladly promised to remember him. Then

the chief baker told his dream, hoping that Joseph would be able to give him good news too. He said that in his dream he had three baskets on his head. In the top one were all kinds of pastries Pharaoh liked, but the birds came and ate them.

Joseph knew at once the meaning of this dream, but he didn't like to tell it. "The three baskets," he said, "are three days. Within three days Pharaoh will lift off your head and hang you on a tree. And the birds will eat away your flesh."

Poor chief baker! There was no smile on his face now.

"Now the third day was Pharaoh's birthday, and he gave a feast for all his officials. He lifted up the heads of the chief cupbearer and the chief baker in the presence of his officials: He restored the chief cupbearer to his position, . . . but he hanged the chief baker, just as Joseph had said to them in his interpretation."

Down in the prison the news soon got around as to what had happened to the chief cupbearer and the chief baker. Joseph must have marveled how exactly his interpretations of the two dreams had come true. He kept wondering and wondering if the chief cupbearer would talk to Pharaoh about him, and have him set free. But month after month passed, and no word came. The chief cupbearer had forgotten all about him!

Poor Joseph! He had to stay in that prison another two whole years.

From the Dungeon
to the Throne

(Genesis 41:1-43)

ONE DAY as Joseph was working in the prison, a messenger came hurrying from the court. "Pharaoh wants to see you at once," he said.

"Me! What for?" I can hear Joseph saying.

"Come at once," repeated the messenger.

How excited Joseph must have felt! Quickly he shaved and changed his clothes. All the way from the prison to the palace he must have asked himself, *What does this mean? Why has he called for me? What have I done wrong now?*

Could it be that the chief cupbearer remembered him at last? That is exactly what had happened. The night before, Pharaoh had had a strange dream that worried him. He felt sure it had an important meaning, but he couldn't think what it might be.

In the morning he had "sent for all the magicians and wise men of Egypt," but none of them were able to interpret the dream.

That's when the chief cupbearer had seen a chance to get a

57

little glory for himself by mentioning Joseph. While the magicians and the wise men were standing around trying to think up some explanation of Pharaoh's dream, he told the king what had happened to him in the prison two years earlier. He described how Joseph's interpretation of his dream and the chief baker's dream had turned out exactly right.

Pharaoh had been interested. Anxious to have his own dream explained, he had sent for Joseph.

Now the great door into the spacious throne room opened, and Joseph was led in. Pharaoh was seated on his golden throne with gorgeously dressed officers and other servants around him. It was an impressive sight to Joseph after all the years he had spent in the drab and dirty prison.

Bowing low to Pharaoh, he waited respectfully to find out why he had been summoned so suddenly.

"I had a dream," said Pharaoh, "and no one can interpret it. But I have heard it said of you that when you hear a dream you can interpret it."

"I cannot do it," said Joseph humbly, "but God will give Pharaoh the answer he desires."

Then Pharaoh told him about his two dreams. In one he had seen seven thin cows that ate up seven fat cows and in the other seven withered heads of grain that ate up seven good heads.

Joseph understood at once, and in a few words he told Pharaoh what the dreams meant. Both dreams, he said, had the same meaning. God had sent them to warn Pharaoh of a com-

ing great famine. There would be seven years of plenty, with
wonderful harvests and lots of grain and other foods. But after
that would come seven years of the worst famine Egypt had ever
seen.

"And now," said Joseph, "let Pharaoh look for a discerning
and wise man and put him in charge of the land of Egypt. Let
Pharaoh appoint commissioners over the land. . . . They should
collect all the food of these good years that are coming and store
up the grain under the authority of Pharaoh, to be kept in the
cities for food. This food should be held in reserve for the
country, to be used during the seven years of famine that will
come upon Egypt, so that the country may not be ruined by the
famine."

Pharaoh was impressed, not only by the interpretation of
his dream but also by this good advice from the fine young man
before him. Turning to his counselors, he said, "Can we find

59

anyone like this man, one in whom is the spirit of God?"

So Pharaoh appointed Joseph to be ruler over all the land of Egypt. "Only with respect to the throne," said Pharaoh, "will I be greater than you."

"Then Pharaoh took his signet ring from his finger and put it on Joseph's finger. He dressed him in robes of fine linen and put a gold chain around his neck. He had him ride in a chariot as his second-in-command, and men shouted before him, 'Make way!' Thus he put him in charge of the whole land of Egypt."

If only Joseph's brothers could have seen him now! They had sold him as a slave, thinking to hurt and humble him. Here he was, riding in the royal chariot through Egypt's cities, with everybody bowing to him!

That's how God works for those who love and trust Him. He overrules the plans of their enemies and makes everything come out right in the end.

If you ever find yourself in a dungeon of some sort, don't be afraid. Be faithful, be true. Somewhere beyond the dungeon is a palace and a throne, and God will lead you there.

Noblest of All

(Genesis 41:45-57; 42; 43:1-14)

THE NEXT few years were very happy ones for Joseph. It must have seemed to him as though he had come out of a long, dark tunnel into a world of sunshine.

Not only did Pharaoh give him a lovely home, a splendid chariot, and a beautiful wife, but the people of Egypt loved him. They thought he was the most wonderful governor they had ever had. They had never been so well off. For seven years in a row, they had the greatest harvests they could remember. "The land produced plentifully."

When the government collected one fifth of all the crops, nobody grumbled. They had so much they didn't know what to do with it all, and no one was worried about the future.

But Joseph knew what was coming. He drove all over the country in his chariot arranging for the storage of the grain. In every city he built storehouses and filled them to the bursting point.

At first he tried to count all the bushels of grain that were brought in, but he finally gave up. "Joseph stored up huge quantities of grain, like the sand of the sea; it was so much that he stopped keeping records because it was beyond measure."

Suddenly the seven good years ended. In the eighth year, when the time came to reap the fields, there was almost no crop at all. Everything was dried up. The seven years of famine had begun.

Everywhere the harvests failed, and soon millions of people were facing starvation. "And all the countries came to Egypt to buy grain from Joseph, because the famine was severe in all the world."

Joseph held on to his stores of grain as long as he could, because he knew they must last for many years. But finally conditions became so bad that he decided to open his storehouses and sell the grain to the hungry people. How glad they were then that he had been so wise and careful!

In Canaan, Jacob was beginning to get worried. During his long life he had never seen a drought like this. There was no grass for his cattle and no grain to make bread for his large family. His harvests had failed too, and now his supplies of food were getting dangerously low.

At last he called his sons together and said to them, "I have heard that there is grain in Egypt. Go down there and buy some for us, so that we may live and not die."

So 10 of his sons set out for Egypt, leaving only Benjamin behind.

They followed the same trail that Joseph had traveled some

20 years before, when they had sold him as a slave to the Ishmaelites. Many times they must have thought about the wrong they had done to him and wondered if they would meet him in Egypt, if indeed he was still alive. But one thing they did not expect—to find him the chief man in Egypt next to Pharaoh.

When they arrived in Egypt, they asked where they could buy grain and were told they first had to get permission from the governor. So they went to see him and bowed low before him. They never imagined for a moment that this important man, dressed in the splendid robes of a high Egyptian official and speaking the Egyptian language, was their own brother.

But Joseph recognized them. He was glad to see them, too! But before letting them know who he was, he decided to find out if they had changed at all during the years since they had sold him into slavery.

In a loud, harsh voice, he accused them of being spies. This frightened them badly, and very humbly they replied that they were not spies. They were just sons of an old man in the land of

63

Canaan; all they wanted was food. But Joseph kept on saying, "You are spies!"

Finally he put them in prison for three days. Perhaps this was to let them see what a prison was like, or maybe he just needed time to think about what to do next. What he wanted most was to see his younger brother again, his own dear Benjamin. But how should he arrange to do this?

Finally Joseph thought of a plan and sent for his brothers. He suggested that one of them remain in prison while the rest took what grain they needed, returned home, and came back with Benjamin. They agreed, and he chose Simeon to be the hostage.

As soldiers bound Simeon, the others looked on, trembling. Suddenly the brothers began to wonder whether all this trouble had come to them because of the way they had treated Joseph so long ago.

They said to one another, "Surely we are being punished because of our brother. We saw how distressed he was when he pleaded with us for his life, but we would not listen; that's why this distress has come upon us." Reuben replied, "Didn't I tell you not to sin against the boy? But you wouldn't listen!"

Though they didn't know it, Joseph understood every word they said. He was so moved by their sorrow for what they had

done to him that "he turned away from them and began to weep." Dear, tenderhearted Joseph!

When they got back home, the brothers found all the money they had paid for the grain inside their sacks. They couldn't understand how it could have gotten there, and it made them more afraid than before to return to Egypt. They didn't know that Joseph, out of his love for them, had ordered that their money should be returned to them.

They told Jacob all that had happened. They explained that the governor of Egypt had said that they could have no more grain unless they took their youngest brother back with them.

"Benjamin!" cried Jacob. " 'Never! Joseph is no more and Simeon is no more, and now you want to take Benjamin. Everything is against me!' "

Again and again Jacob refused to let Benjamin go to Egypt, but at last, when all their food was gone, he had to give in.

"Take your brother also," he said sadly, "and go. . . . And may God Almighty grant you mercy before the man so that he will let your other brother and Benjamin come back with you. As for me, if I am bereaved, I am bereaved."

Poor Jacob! He had already lost Joseph. Simeon was in prison in Egypt, and now he was afraid he was going to lose Benjamin, too. How God must have smiled when He thought of the surprise that was just around the corner.

Family Reunion

(Genesis 43:1-47:27)

THE FOOD supply was getting very low in Jacob's household when his sons set out for Egypt once more. This time, they took Benjamin and double the money with them besides a gift for the governor.

Joseph was expecting them. He knew they would have to return for more food, and when word reached him that they were in the city, he decided to give them the surprise of their lives. He sent them an invitation to have dinner at his house.

Dinner with the governor! They were more frightened than ever. "It's because of the money that was in our sacks," they said to one another. "Now he is going to punish us and take us for slaves."

But they were mistaken. When they saw Joseph, he asked, "How is your aged father you told me about? Is he still living?"

"Your servant our father is still alive and well," they replied, again bowing low before him.

Suddenly Joseph caught sight of Benjamin. He was so moved at seeing his little brother again that he hurried out of the room and burst into tears. How he longed to throw his arms around him, but he didn't dare do it yet.

Joseph washed his face and returned to the dining hall. Calmly, he ordered the meal to be served. He ate by himself at a separate table. His Egyptian officers sat at a second table, and his brothers, at another.

They "looked at each other in astonishment," the Bible says. The meal was magnificent, but that could be expected at the governor's table. What they couldn't understand was how they happened to be seated in order of their ages and why Benjamin's plate was heaped with five times as much food as anyone else's. But still they didn't guess who the governor was!

Then Joseph played one more trick on them. He gave orders that when their sacks were filled with grain again, his own silver cup was to be placed in Benjamin's sack.

At last the brothers set off for home, proud of having been invited to dinner with the governor of Egypt and very happy that everything had turned out so well after all. But soon they

heard the sound of galloping horses. Looking around, they were horrified to find that it was the governor's steward with a bodyguard.

Angrily the steward accused them of stealing the governor's special silver cup.

"Why would we do anything like that?" the brothers asked. "We even brought back the silver we found in our sacks from the last time we were here." They declared that if anyone had the cup, he would die.

"Very well," the steward said. "The man won't need to die, but I'll take him for my slave." He searched each man's sack, and found the cup, of course, in Benjamin's.

What a sad journey that was back to the city. All the joy of the morning was gone, and they were filled with new fears. They couldn't go home without Benjamin. Back at the governor's palace, they fell on their faces before Joseph. Judah pleaded with him, describing his father's grief at losing one of his sons, who he thought had been torn to pieces.

"Now then," Judah begged, "please let your servant remain here as my lord's slave in place of the boy, and let the boy return with his brothers. How can I go back to my father if the boy is not with me? No! Do not let me see the misery that would come upon my father."

This was more than Joseph could stand. He knew now that his brothers had changed since they had sold him into slavery. They really cared about their father's grief and about what happened to Benjamin. Suddenly Joseph raised his voice in command, saying, "Have everyone except these brothers leave!"

"So there was no one with Joseph when he made himself

known to his brothers. And he wept so loudly that the Egyptians heard him, and Pharaoh's household heard about it."

At first the brothers wondered what all this meant. Then, when Joseph was able to control himself, he said, "I am Joseph!"

Joseph! Could this be Joseph? If it were, what would he do to them in revenge for all they had made him suffer? His brothers were terrified.

But Joseph's heart harbored no revenge. Only love. He had forgiven them long ago, and all he wanted was to be friends again.

In their fear they had moved away from him, but he said, ever so gently, "Come close to me."

"When they had done so, he said, 'I am your brother Joseph, the one you sold into Egypt! And now, do not be distressed and do not be angry with yourselves for selling me here, because it was to save lives that God sent me ahead of you. For two years now there has been famine in the land, and for the next five years there will not be plowing and reaping. But God sent me ahead of you to preserve for you a remnant on earth and to save your lives by a great deliverance. So then, it was not you who sent me here, but God.' "

How kindly he tried to take away all their worry! He didn't

want them to blame themselves for what had happened. It was God who had sent him to Egypt, he said. Only a truly noble person could speak like that!

Then he told them of his plan to bring the whole family into the land of Goshen, a section of Egypt, where he could supply them with food through the five years of famine still to come.

"I will provide for you there," he said. "Otherwise you and your household and all who belong to you will become destitute."

There wasn't a trace of meanness in Joseph's character. Although he was powerful and wealthy, he never once thought of trying to get even with these men who had treated him so cruelly.

"Then he threw his arms around his brother Benjamin and wept, and Benjamin embraced him, weeping. And he kissed all his brothers and wept over them."

Yes, he kissed them all. Reuben, Simeon, Judah—every one, even those who had actually thrown him into the pit and sold him into slavery. He kissed them! What love! What forgiveness! How pleased God must have been with his greatness of spirit!

"When the news reached Pharaoh's palace that Joseph's

brothers had come, Pharaoh and all his officials were pleased."

"Bring your father and your families back to me," Pharaoh told Joseph. "I will give you the best of the land of Egypt." He also gave Joseph's brothers some carts, so the women and children and Joseph's old father could travel in comfort.

As a parting gift Joseph gave each of his brothers a set of new clothes, and he gave Benjamin "three hundred shekels of silver and five sets of clothes." To his father he sent "ten donkeys loaded with the best things of Egypt, and ten female donkeys loaded with grain and bread and other provisions for his journey."

Joseph tried to think of everything that would make them happy and at ease. Then with a smile, remembering their old weakness, he told them, "Don't quarrel on the way!"

When the brothers reached home, they all trooped into their old father's tent. "Joseph is still alive! In fact, he is ruler of all Egypt," they cried.

Jacob wouldn't believe them. It didn't seem possible. Why, the dear boy had been dead more than 20 years.

"He isn't dead," they kept on saying. "He's alive. We saw him and talked with him." They then told him what had happened and all that Joseph had said to them. Still the old man wouldn't believe them.

They took him outside and showed him the carts loaded with good things that only Joseph's loving heart could have provided. Then Jacob knew the story must be true. A smile came over his face, and a new light shone in his eyes. "I'm convinced!" he cried, "My son Joseph is still alive. I will go and see him before I die."

No one lost any time in getting everything ready for the journey, Jacob least of all. He had just one thought—that soon he would see his precious Joseph again.

As the caravan paused at Beersheba, Jacob offered sacrifices of joy and thanksgiving to God. That night God spoke to him, saying, "Jacob, Jacob."

And he said, "Here I am."

" 'I am God, the God of your father,' he said. 'Do not be afraid to go down to Egypt. . . . I will surely bring you back again. And Joseph's own hand will close your eyes.' "

Cheered by this kindly message, Jacob went on his way with new courage. "And Israel's sons took their father Jacob and their children and their wives in the carts that Pharaoh had sent to transport him.

"They also took with them their livestock and the possessions they had acquired in Canaan, and Jacob and all his offspring went to Egypt."

How happy and excited Joseph must have been when news reached him that his father was nearing Egypt! The Bible tells us that "Joseph had his chariot made ready and went to Goshen to meet his father Israel. As soon as Joseph appeared before him, he threw his arms around his father and wept for a long time.

"Israel said to Joseph, 'Now I am ready to die, since I have seen for myself that you are still alive.' "

But he didn't die. He lived another 17 years!

"Now the Israelites settled in Egypt in the region of Goshen. They acquired property there and were fruitful and increased greatly in number."

So we see how God used one godly boy to save thousands of people from starvation. Through Joseph, Eve's "offspring" was once again preserved, and the name of the God of heaven, the God of Joseph, and the God of Israel was made known in all the world.

72

PART TWO

Stories of

Israel in Egypt

(Exodus 1:1-10:29)

Light in the Darkness

(Genesis 50:22-26; Exodus 1:1-14)

"GRANDPA, will we ever see the beautiful land you keep telling us about?"

"Someday," said Joseph, "some happy day."

The slave boy who became governor of Egypt was now more than 100 years old. He was a grandfather of Ephraim's children and the great-uncle of a host of boys and girls belonging to the families of his 11 brothers.

I can see these children running into his palace to talk to him, because his kind, gentle heart made everyone love him. And what wonderful stories he told! They loved to hear him talk about the old days when he was a boy in Canaan. They could almost see the green hills, snowcapped mountains, and rushing waterfalls that he described. Canaan was their homeland, too, though they had never seen it and could only dream about it.

Joseph longed to go back to Canaan but never could. He didn't have time. He was always too busy with his many duties and later was too old to travel.

75

God's people, who had moved to Egypt, built homes there and were very happy during the life of Joseph, for God had prospered him and made him a wise ruler under Pharaoh.

Then one sad day Joseph felt that death was near. Calling his family to him for the last time, he said, "I am about to die. But God will surely come to your aid and take you up out of this land to the land he promised on oath to Abraham, Isaac and Jacob. . . . Then you must carry my bones up from this place."

Joseph knew that God did not plan for them always to live in a heathen nation. Someday, somehow, God would lead them back to the beautiful land He had promised to give to them. And Joseph wanted to go along too. That is why he said, "Carry my bones." If he couldn't go back to Canaan when he was alive, at least he would rest there in death.

The family promised to remember his dying wish, and Joseph, contented, breathed his last. The Bible does not tell us anything about his funeral, but it must have been very splendid. No doubt a great procession with thousands of people followed the body of the kind, wise governor to its resting place.

His tomb may well have been near the pyramids, where so many of the great men of Egypt had been buried. For years passers-by would say, "There lies one of the finest leaders this country ever knew."

In a few years, however, "a new king, who did not know about Joseph, came to power in Egypt." This king was concerned that there now seemed to be more Israelites than Egyptians in Goshen, and he didn't like it. The other Egyptians didn't like it either. They grumbled about the Israelites' owning the finest land and holding important positions in the government.

Having listened to one complaint after another, Pharaoh decided that something must be done. He called his counselors together. " 'Look,' he said to his people, 'the Israelites have become much too numerous for us. Come, we must deal shrewdly with them or they will become even more numerous and, if war breaks out, will join our enemies, fight against us and leave the country.' "

This was just the chance the counselors had been waiting for. They worked out a cruel plan that would give them control of the Hebrews. No longer would the Israelites be treated as equals, but as slaves. They would not be allowed to work for themselves or for their own profit. They would have to work for the Egyptians.

Imagine how the children of Israel must have felt as news of Pharaoh's decree spread among them! I can almost hear them saying, "Slavery! How could they make us slaves?"

But that is exactly what had happened. Suddenly they realized that the good old days under Joseph's kindly rule had gone forever. Now they were told what to do and were kicked and beaten if they failed to obey. The Egyptians "put slave

masters over them to oppress them with forced labor, and they built Pithom and Rameses as store cities for Pharaoh."

Day after day they worked in the blazing heat. From sunrise to sunset Joseph's descendants made bricks, mixed mortar, and built walls, while the slave masters stood by, whips in their hands, ready to punish anyone who tried to rest.

Although the Egyptians made the lives of the Hebrews "bitter with hard labor," they could not break their spirit. The Israelites often felt sad and discouraged, but hope never left their hearts. And the more Pharaoh tried to make life hard for them, "the more they multiplied and spread."

Back in their homes at night they would talk about God's promise to Abraham, which had been handed down from one generation to the next for many, many years. "Know for certain that your descendants will be strangers in a country not their own, and they will be enslaved and mistreated four hundred years. . . . In the fourth generation your descendants will come back here."

Again and again they must have tried to figure out when the time would be up and which was the "fourth generation." Often they must have cried in their trouble, "How long, O Lord, how long?"

Then someone would pass by Joseph's tomb and remember his promise: "God will surely come to your aid" and take you up out of this land. Once more light would break through the darkness, hope would rise, and hearts would be brave again. 🖋

Baby to the Rescue

(Exodus 1:15-2:10)

A S PHARAOH rode out in his chariot one day to inspect his two new treasure cities, Pithom and Rameses, he saw something that worried him at first, then made him angry.

He had never seen so many Hebrews in all his life. They were in the fields and all around the brick ovens. They were unloading blocks of stone from barges on the river and hauling other blocks into place on the houses and temples they were building. They were everywhere.

Worst of all, every one of them looked so strong and healthy! He had thought he would kill them off with hard labor, but now there were more of them than ever. His plan had not worked.

Pharaoh decided that if he could not get rid of the Hebrews by working them to death, he would do it some other way. What could be easier than killing their infants as soon as they were born? So Pharaoh decreed that every baby boy must be thrown into the Nile River.

When the Hebrew fathers and mothers heard the dreadful news, their faces turned pale. At first they could hardly believe it. No ruler could be so cruel as to order that all baby boys should be murdered like this!

But it *was* true. Soon terror filled the hearts of all as they heard stories about Egyptians taking babies away from their mothers and flinging them into the Nile to drown or be eaten by crocodiles. Imagine how the people must have felt in homes where a baby was on the way or had just arrived! Imagine how the older brothers and sisters must have worried themselves sick, to say nothing of the fathers and mothers.

This was Israel's darkest hour. They had put up with the long hours of work and the merciless acts of the slave masters, but this cold-blooded killing of their children was too much to bear. It made them want to leave Egypt more than ever. They began to pray for help as they had never prayed before, and they wanted it *now*.

At this very moment, when things seemed as though they could not get worse, God sent a baby to the rescue.

It happened this way. One day a baby boy was born to Amram and Jochebed. These godly Hebrews had a little girl called Miriam and a little boy named Aaron, and they had wanted another little boy so much. But now! Oh, dear! What if the soldiers should find him?

80

Nobody knows for sure what name the parents gave their new baby. Maybe it was Abraham or Enoch or Joseph. Whatever it was, it became lost. Later on, as we shall see, he was given another name, and this one stuck to him for life.

Jochebed was a loving mother, and she made up her mind that the Egyptians would not get her baby, not if she could help it. Somehow or other she managed to keep him hidden for three months, but it's pretty hard to hide 3-month-old babies anywhere. Just think of the noise they make when they cry!

One day, when Jochebed knew she could not keep her secret any longer, she got a bright idea. She would make a little boat, put the baby in it, and float it near the riverbank. Perhaps—who could tell?—some kindhearted Egyptian woman passing by might find it and feel sorry for the poor little thing inside.

Jochebed took a desperate chance, but it seemed to be the only way out. It was better than doing nothing. Any moment someone might burst into the house and snatch away her baby.

Jochebed wove a basket with reeds from the river, making

it watertight by coating it with tar. Then she fixed a soft little bed inside and tenderly—oh, so tenderly!—laid her baby in it. She kissed him goodbye, closed the lid, and carried the basket to the riverbank.

With a breaking heart and tears running down her cheeks, she placed it gently among the marsh plants. Then, leaving Miriam to watch what would happen, she went home and asked God to protect her child.

Miriam was not alone on that riverbank. Angels were there, too, watching with her. This was a special baby for whom God had planned a very wonderful future.

After a while, who should walk by but Pharaoh's daughter, with some of her maids. Suddenly she caught sight of the strange oblong basket in the rushes, and sent one of her maids to carry it to her. Lifting the lid, the princess saw a beautiful baby boy inside, and the poor little thing was crying.

"This is one of the Hebrew babies," she said. Perhaps she

picked him up and loved him. The Bible says she "felt sorry for him." At least she wasn't cruel and hardhearted like her father.

As her maids crowded around to look at the baby, wondering what to do with him, Miriam came running up. It must have taken a lot of courage for her to speak to the princess, but with her baby brother's life in danger, she was ready to do anything.

"Please, ma'am," she said, "shall I go and get one of the Hebrew women to nurse the baby for you?"

Pharaoh's daughter was relieved. This seemed to be a good way out of a very awkward situation. "Yes, go," she said. So Miriam ran like the wind to find her mother.

"Mother, Mother!" I can hear her gasping as she rushed into the house. "Come quickly, come quickly! The princess has found baby brother!"

How long do you suppose it took Jochebed to get from her house to the riverbank? Not very long. She had never run so

fast in her life. When she saw the princess and her maids and the baby crying for his dinner, she was so happy she didn't know whether to laugh or to cry. Of course, she tried to keep a straight face so the princess wouldn't think that she was the child's mother.

Then the princess spoke to her, and she could hardly believe her ears. "Take this baby," she said gently, "and nurse him for me, and I will pay you."

The way Jochebed took the baby and cuddled it was enough to give her away, but if the princess guessed the truth, she didn't say anything. As she left with her maids for the palace, Jochebed and Miriam hurried happily home. Their hearts were overflowing with thankfulness to God for the way He had saved their precious little boy.

It was all too wonderful to believe. Not only did they have their baby back, but no one could ever kill him now. He belonged to the princess, and she was going to pay his own mother to take care of him! She could give him the best food, the best care, and Pharaoh's daughter would pay for it!

If the princess had known who this child would be someday and what he would do, would she have saved his life? I don't know. Perhaps she would have. This baby was the very one God had sent to lead His people out of Egypt to freedom.

Training a Prince

(Exodus 2:10; Acts 7:20-23)

JOCHEBED was glad to have her baby back safe and sound. As she thought over what had happened down by the river, she realized that her baby didn't really belong to her anymore. Her own little baby had a new mother. Someday the princess would send for him, and take him away, and never give him back again. He would not grow up to be Jochebed's child, a Hebrew; he would be a prince of Egypt.

"How long will I be able to keep him?" she must have asked herself again and again. One year, two years, 10 years? She didn't know. But she made up her mind that during the time she was allowed to keep him, whether it was long or short, she would give him the very best training she could.

Jochebed knew that her son would meet many temptations in the palace, so she tried to anchor his little heart to God. She taught him to pray and to sing songs of praise. She told him the story of Creation and the Fall. She talked about God's plan of salvation, that sweet and beautiful story that had been handed down from parent to child from the days of Adam and Eve.

God, she taught him, is a holy God who expects all His children to be good and pure and loyal. Those who want to be truly happy will follow His teachings and obey His laws. She told him about the history of his people and how God had promised Abraham that someday they would all be delivered from slavery and taken back to Canaan. She also told him about his own wonderful rescue from death and that she believed God had a wonderful plan for his life if he stayed true and loyal to Him.

All too quickly the years went by. Then one day, when her boy was 12 years old, the dreaded message arrived. The princess wanted her son brought to the palace at once.

What a sad day! Mother choked back her sobs as she packed up the few things he would need to take along with him. Father blinked back his tears. Miriam cried her heart out. Aaron looked glum, not sure whether to be sad or envious.

Perhaps some soldiers came in a chariot to get him. I don't know. Maybe the family walked to the palace and stood together outside before the gates swung open. The boy's heart would have been full of questioning, and the parents' hearts would have been full of fears and sadness. Then came the last goodbyes, the last promises to remember and love forever.

When the guards took the youngster inside and the gates closed behind him, the great palace must have seemed to be a

very lonely place to him. His new mother must have tried to be especially kind to him, but somehow it wasn't the same. The princess also gave him a new name. She said it would be Moses, which meant "son" in Egyptian and "drawn out" in the Hebrew language. Perhaps Moses cried himself to sleep that night, thinking that he would never return to his home and dear ones again.

But with the morning came new interests. Everywhere Moses turned he saw wonderful things. Life here was so different from everything he had known in the humble little cottage that had been his home until now.

The Bible tells us that he was "no ordinary child," and he was soon a favorite in the court. Everybody loved him. The best teachers in the country tutored him in mathematics, law, medicine, military science, and many other things. As time went by, Moses became "educated in all the wisdom of the Egyptians and was powerful in speech and action."

Moses soon reached the prime of life. His body was strong, and his mind was keen. He already had the qualities of a great leader. He could ride a horse or drive a chariot with skill and daring. He had learned his lessons so well that he knew a lot about the history, geography, and religion of Egypt.

All the court—in fact, all Egypt—knew that here was a young man of unusual gifts who would be able to take Pharaoh's place someday. And Moses himself was aware that he was in

direct line to the throne. Someday, if he wanted to, he could become ruler of Egypt.

Yet with all his studies and busy life in the royal court, Moses never forgot the things his mother had told him in his boyhood. Every day he thought about God and what Mother had said God wanted him to be and to do. As the years slipped by he felt more and more out of place in the palace. Deep loyalties, which court life could not change, drew him toward his people.

The Hebrews were suffering more all the time. Moses heard reports of the terrible way the Hebrew slaves were being treated, and he often wondered how he could help them. If he revealed that he was not an Egyptian after all, but belonged to the very people the Egyptians despised, he would lose his position and his chance for the throne. What should he do?

When Moses said his prayers, he talked with God about it all, asking Him to make clear what he should do. Then one night he made his decision—"He chose to be mistreated along with the people of God rather than to enjoy the pleasures of sin for a short time. He regarded disgrace for the sake of Christ as of greater value than the treasures of Egypt." *

It was a big choice to make, and it proved to be a turning point in the history of Israel and of the world.

---

* Hebrews 11:25, 26.

Flight for Life

(Exodus 2:11-21; Acts 7:24-29)

A S A PRINCE of Egypt and the pride and joy of his royal mother, Moses had everything a young man could wish for. Lots of money, a beautiful home, many servants, chariots, and horses—they were all his.

Because of his position, people fussed over him, flattered him, and ran to do whatever he asked them. It was enough to turn any boy's head, and it would have been surprising if Moses hadn't had a pretty high opinion of himself and of what he could do.

As he thought about the suffering of his people, he planned one scheme after another to set them free. Perhaps this would work, or that. But he had one great lesson to learn: When his people were rescued, it would be through God's power, not his.

No one in the court had any idea what was going on in his mind, of course. No one doubted his loyalty to Pharaoh. They would have been shocked if they had known that he had decided to defend the Hebrew slaves and try to free them.

So no one was concerned when one day he left the palace,

climbed into his chariot, and rode out to a section of the country where the Hebrews were working. People bowed and smiled at him, as they always did when they saw their handsome young prince.

Leaving the city behind him, he found himself on a lonely, deserted stretch of road where he saw something that sickened him. One of the Egyptian slave drivers was cruelly beating a Hebrew slave. Looking this way and that to make sure that no one was watching, Moses leaped from his chariot, strode over to the bully, and knocked him to the ground, killing him.

The poor Hebrew, astonished to see a prince of the royal house striking one of the king's men, ran as fast as he could to tell the news to his people. Meanwhile Moses was left with the body of the man he had killed. Not wanting the Hebrews—or himself—to be accused of murdering an officer, he decided to bury the body in the sand.

As Moses returned to the palace he felt rather pleased with himself. He had made a good start. He felt sure that when the Hebrews heard of what he had done, they would be glad that they had a friend at court who was willing to help them. He never dreamed they would betray him. "Moses thought that his own people would realize that God was using him to rescue them, but they did not."

Confident that all was going well, he went out again the next day to see what he could do for his people. This time he came across two Hebrews fighting together. The stronger one

91

← PAINTING BY HARRY ANDERSON

Although Moses was the adopted son of Pharaoh's daughter, he loved his own people, and because he could not stand to see them abused, he forsook the royal courts to go into exile.

was beating the other man without mercy.

Moses was surprised and disappointed. How could he help his people if they fought among themselves? "Men," he called to them, "you are brothers; why do you want to hurt each other?"

He hoped that he could help them be friends and that they would thank him for his good advice. Instead, as Moses tried to separate them, the man who was doing the beating turned on him and said, "Who made *you* ruler and judge over us? Do you want to kill me as you killed the Egyptian yesterday?"

Moses was shocked. This man already knew what Moses had done the day before! He had buried the body, but not the deed. If this unfriendly Hebrew knew about it, all Egypt must know about it too. Perhaps even Pharaoh had heard.

Anxiously Moses hurried back to the palace. Here he found that his worst fears were true. Everybody was talking about him and what he had done. Somehow the news had been flashed all over the country that Prince Moses had killed one of the king's officers for beating a Hebrew slave!

Pharaoh, he learned, was very angry. Such an act was unpardonable and must be punished by death. An order had

92

already gone out for his arrest and execution.

How Moses escaped we do not know. Maybe some friends helped him, or perhaps the princess used her power to protect him. Somehow he managed to escape without getting caught.

The safest place to go, he thought, was the land of Midian. Nobody would know him there, and he could hide until this whole sorry affair had been forgotten.

Moses must have started out on his journey with a very heavy heart. As he saw the pyramids of Egypt gradually fading out of sight behind him, he knew that life would never be the same. Gone forever were the easy days in the palace. From now on he would be a lonely, homeless exile.

And worst of all was the thought of the foolish mistake he had made. He should never have killed that Egyptian. He had acted rashly. He should have taken more time to work out his plans. He had spoiled his chance to help his people. Now who would deliver them?

Day after day Moses dragged his weary feet over the hot, dry sand of the desert. Night after night he slept in the open, his eyes wet with tears at the thought of the mess he had made.

At last he came to Midian and sat down by a well. In the early evening, he saw seven young girls coming toward him. After the loneliness of the desert they must have been a very welcome sight.

He learned that they were sisters, daughters of Jethro, an important man in that part of the country. As the girls began to draw water from the well for the sheep they had with them, some rough shepherds arrived and tried to drive them away.

This was too much for Moses, who had been trained in courtesy at home and in the court. Gallantly he stood up for the girls and told the shepherds to behave themselves. Then he drew water from the well himself and poured it into the troughs for the sheep to drink. This was a strange thing for a prince of Egypt to do, but it was the first happy moment he'd had in a long time.

When the sheep were watered, the seven girls thanked him, said goodbye, and hurried home. When they arrived, their father asked them why they were back so much earlier than usual. They said it was because an Egyptian had defended them against the shepherds and had watered the flock.

"And where is he?" asked Jethro. "Why did you leave him? Invite him to have something to eat."

So the seven girls came trooping back to the well and apologized to Moses for leaving him there so ungraciously. Then they took him back home with them, and that's where Moses lived for many years, until he had learned the lesson God wanted to teach him.

It took exactly as long for him to learn this lesson in the wisdom of God as it had taken him to become "educated in all the wisdom of the Egyptians."

Voice in the Desert

(Exodus 2:21-4:27)

YEAR after year went by. Moses married Zipporah, one of the seven girls he had met at the well. They had two children. The first he called Gershom, meaning perhaps "a stranger here," because he had been "an alien in a foreign land." The second he called Eliezer, meaning "my God is a help"—a very lovely thought behind a boy's name.

One day news reached them that the Pharaoh who had threatened to kill Moses was dead. This was good news, but the rest was bad. Things were no better for the children of Israel. Their slavery was as cruel as ever.

If Moses ever wondered whether he should return to Egypt and try to help his people, he gave up on the idea at once. "How can I help them now?" he asked himself. "I have no power or influence anymore. Everybody has forgotten me. If I were to go back now, they wouldn't even recognize me."

Moses was now ready to admit that *he* could not deliver Israel. Years ago he had thought that maybe he could. Now he knew he could not. And when he had finally learned this

Russ Harlan

lesson, God could use him.

Eighty years had passed since the princess had found him in the little basket. The first 40 years he had spent in Egypt, where he learned "the wisdom of the Egyptians." The next 40 he had spent as a shepherd in Midian, unlearning much of what he had learned before.

He was no longer a proud young prince. He was old—and perhaps a little sad. But he need not have been discouraged, for God had not left him. Every hour of every day since he was born God had watched over him.

Yes, and God still remembered Jochebed's prayers for him and his own determination to do what was right, whatever it cost him. Although Moses didn't realize it, God was still counting on him to lead His people out of slavery into freedom.

Now the time had come. God was ready, and His man was ready. And they met, not in a palace, not beside one of the pyramids, but by a bush in the desert.

Wandering over the barren hills one day, Moses suddenly noticed a strange sight. A bush seemed to be on fire, but it wasn't burning up. He could not explain it and said to himself, "I will go over and see this strange sight—why the bush does not burn up." In all the years he had studied science in Egypt, he had never heard of anything like this.

Then a voice called his name. "Moses! Moses!"

Moses looked around. He could not see anyone. He had thought he was alone in the wilderness. But Somebody was there, very close to him, Somebody who knew his name.

The voice spoke again. " 'Do not come any closer,' God

2-7

← PAINTING BY RUSSELL HARLAN

While tending sheep, Moses was startled to see a bush all afire yet not burning up. When he drew nearer, God spoke to him out of the flames and told him to lead Israel out of Egypt.

said. 'Take off your sandals, for the place where you are standing is holy ground.' "

Now Moses knew that God had come to speak to him. Quickly he took off his sandals and bowed his head. He had been eager to examine the burning bush, but now "he was afraid to look at God."

God said, "I am the God of your father, the God of Abraham, the God of Isaac and the God of Jacob. . . . I have indeed seen the misery of my people in Egypt. I have heard them crying out because of their slave drivers, and I am concerned about their suffering. So I have come down to rescue them."

As Moses listened, his heart was touched by God's compassion for His people. During the 40 years since he had left Egypt, he had almost forgotten what was going on there. But God had not forgotten one sorrow or one tear during all those long, long years.

But why is He telling me? Moses must have thought to himself. *Why has He come to speak to* me *in this wilderness?* He soon found out.

"So now, go," God said. "I am sending you to Pharaoh to bring my people the Israelites out of Egypt."

No, he couldn't go now! At one time he would have been glad to go, but not now. When he was younger, perhaps, but not at 80 years of age. He was too old, too much of a shepherd. "Who am *I*," he said, "that *I* should go to Pharaoh and bring the Israelites out of Egypt?"

Moses had lost all his old self-confidence. And God knew

98

it. At last Moses was ready for the great work God had for him to
do.

"*I* will be with you," God said. "You won't be going alone.
You can trust Me at all times to help you."

But Moses didn't want to go. He began to make excuses. The
people wouldn't believe him, he said. They wouldn't believe that
he had met God in the wilderness.

Patiently God answered all his objections and gave him signs
to convince both him and the people.

"What do you have in your hand?" God asked.

"A staff."

"Throw it on the ground," God said.

Moses did, and his staff became a snake. Startled, he ran away
from it.

"Take it by the tail," said God.

That took courage, but Moses obeyed. The snake became a
staff again!

Next God made Moses' hand white with leprosy and a moment later made it completely well again.

Moses was impressed, but he still was not willing to go. He thought he was "slow of speech" and wouldn't know what to say.

"O Lord," he said, "please send someone else to do it."

But God did not want someone else. He wanted Moses. However, He agreed that his brother Aaron could go with him to give him courage and to do the talking. "I know he can speak well," said God. "He is already on his way to meet you."

This was wonderful news. Aaron was coming to meet him! Why, he hadn't seen his brother for 40 years. How good it would be to see him again!

What Moses didn't know was that God had already spoken to Aaron and said, "Go into the desert to meet Moses."

So the two brothers were on their way—one traveling from Egypt, the other from Midian. Two brothers looking for each other in a great, wide wilderness! However could they hope to meet in such a wild, desolate land?

But they did. They met "at the mountain of God." And there they kissed each other, they were so glad to be together again.

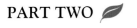

God's Sevenfold Promise

(Exodus 4:28-6:29)

WHAT a lot of things Moses and Aaron had to talk about when they met in the wilderness! They must have talked for hours. Aaron told about everything that had happened in Egypt since Moses had run away from Pharaoh's court. Moses reported to Aaron everything that had happened to him from the day he arrived in Midian until he met God at the burning bush.

"Then Moses told Aaron everything the Lord had sent him to say, and also about all the miraculous signs he had commanded him to perform." As they talked together about how God had spoken to them, they felt sure He was calling them both to do a great work for Him. All they needed to do was obey.

Perhaps there on the mountainside they prayed. They thanked God for the way He had led them through all the long, long years since they had met last, and they asked Him to guide them through the days ahead.

Finally the two old brothers—one 80, the other 83—

started on their way back to Egypt—the land of slavery, tyranny, and tears. As hour after hour they walked along through the wild, desolate country, they talked about what they would do when they got there.

First, they would meet with the leaders of the Israelites and tell them what had happened at the burning bush. If these men believed their story and were convinced that God had promised to rescue them, then they would go to Pharaoh and ask him to set the people free.

When they reached Egypt, they arranged a meeting with the elders of Israel, and "Aaron told them everything the Lord had said to Moses. He also performed the signs before the people."

As the people saw the staff become a snake and Moses' hand become leprous, then healthy again, they were convinced

that both men were telling the truth. And when they heard that God had said, "I am concerned about their suffering. So I have come down to rescue them," they wept for joy and "bowed down and worshiped."

You may be sure that it did not take long for word to get around about what had happened at that meeting. As the news spread from home to home, a great new hope surged up among the Hebrews. God had heard their prayers! He was about to save them! Joseph's promise would soon be fulfilled!

But things did not go too well the next day. When Moses and Aaron met Pharaoh, they found it was not going to be as easy as they had thought to set Israel free. Pharaoh had no

PAINTING BY HERBERT RUDEEN AFTER E. J. POYNTER

intention whatever of letting them go.

Aaron said, " 'This is what the Lord, the God of Israel, says: "Let my people go, so that they may hold a festival to me in the desert." ' "

"Who is the Lord," snorted Pharaoh, "that I should obey him and let Israel go? I do not know the Lord and I will not let Israel go."

This was bad enough, but what happened next was even worse.

When Moses and Aaron explained that all they wanted at the moment was that their people might "take a three-day journey into the desert to offer sacrifices to the Lord," Pharaoh became furious. Whoever heard of such a thing! Slaves asking for a whole week's vacation! Ridiculous! And if they thought they could take time off, they were not working hard enough. So he would give them more to do.

Pharaoh ordered that from now on the people of Israel would not be given straw to mix into their bricks. They would have to gather it themselves and still make the same number of bricks as they had before.

When the Israelites heard about this, they were frightened. How could they make the same number of bricks when they had to spend so much time trying to find straw? It was impossible. And when they failed, the slave drivers beat them cruelly, shouting, "Complete the work required of you for each day, just as when you had straw."

The leaders of Israel finally complained to Pharaoh, but all he said to them was, "Lazy, that's what you are—lazy! That is

104

why you keep saying, 'Let us go and sacrifice to the Lord.' "

Angrily, the Israelites turned on Moses and Aaron. "Look what you have done to us!" they said. "We're worse off than ever. You've picked a nice way to save us from slavery!"

Moses prayed to God. "Why has this happened?" he asked. "Why did You send me? I went to talk to Pharaoh in Your name, but he just made more trouble for Your people. You haven't rescued them at all."

But though Moses was discouraged, God was not. He never is. He always knows what He is going to do next.

"Now you will see what I will do to Pharaoh," God said. "Because of my mighty hand he will let them go; because of my mighty hand he will drive them out of his country."

This was hard for Moses to believe after all that had happened. So God gave him seven promises, which he was to pass on to the children of Israel. Tell them, God said, that "I will bring you out from under the yoke of the Egyptians. I will free you from being slaves to them, and will redeem you. . . . I will take you as my own people, . . . I will be your God. . . . I will bring you to the land I swore with uplifted hand to give to Abraham, . . . I will give it to you as a possession."

Seven times God said it. "I will . . . I will . . . I will."

Moses believed. But the people didn't. When he passed on the seven promises to them, they refused to listen "because of their discouragement and cruel bondage." Their spirits were crushed. Their hopes were dead. Things had never looked so dark to them. But it was just the darkness before the dawn. The time for their deliverance was near.

Frogs in the Palace

(Exodus 7:8-8:32)

A FEW days later Moses and Aaron went to see Pharaoh again. As soon as he saw them he demanded that they work a miracle to prove the power of their God. Aaron threw down his staff in front of Pharaoh, and it became a snake.

The king was impressed, but he wasn't willing to admit that this was a sign of the power of the Hebrews' God. He thought it was just magic. So he called for his own magicians and ordered them to do the same trick.

They did. As soon as their staffs hit the floor, they became snakes. Now there were several snakes crawling all over the place! For a moment it looked as though Moses and Aaron were nothing more than two smart magicians.

But then a strange thing happened. Aaron's staff slithered up to one of the other snakes and swallowed it. Then it went after another and another, until it had swallowed them all. When the last one had disappeared, Aaron took his snake by the tail, and it became a staff again.

FROGS IN THE PALACE

It was all very mysterious. Again Pharaoh was impressed, especially since his magicians looked very silly without their staffs. But he hardened his heart and refused to do what Moses and Aaron wanted.

The next day, as Pharaoh went down to the Nile, perhaps for his morning bath, he found Moses and Aaron waiting for him on the riverbank. Pharaoh must have been very annoyed to see them again so soon and in such a place. And when Aaron began to call to him in a loud voice, Pharaoh must have gotten very angry. But he stopped and listened. What was the old man saying? They were strange words from a Hebrew slave. "This is what the Lord says: By this you will know that I am the Lord: With the staff that is in my hand I will strike the water of the Nile, and it will be changed into blood."

The man must be crazy! thought Pharaoh. *Does he think he can turn the waters of the Nile into blood?*

But just then Pharaoh smelled something dreadful coming from the river. Turning to see what was the matter, he saw that the water had turned a dull red color. Dead fish were rising to the surface and washing up at his feet. It was a terrible sight. Sickened, he "turned and went into his palace" while "all the Egyptians dug along the Nile to get drinking water."

Pharaoh called his magicians and ordered them to turn water into blood. They did. Not the Nile, of course, but enough water to convince Pharaoh that Moses and Aaron were just using some special magic. No! he would not listen to them, and he would not let Israel go.

Then came the frogs, millions and millions of them. They swarmed all over Egypt. They jumped through the open doors and windows of the people's homes until nobody knew what to do with them. They hopped into Pharaoh's palace, into his bedroom, even up onto his bed. They leaped into his kitchen, into the ovens, and into the dough that the baker was making into bread for him to eat.

Once again Pharaoh called for his magicians, and once again they copied what Moses and Aaron had done. Now there were even more frogs hopping around than before!

Pharaoh simply could not get away from the frogs. He stepped on them, sat on them, slept on them. He ordered his servants to kill them, but the more they killed, the more there seemed to be. There was no end to them!

The Egyptians had seen swarms of frogs before, but never so many. They began to complain to Pharaoh, but he could not do anything to help them.

At last, unable to stand it any longer, he sent for Moses and Aaron. "Pray to the Lord to take the frogs away, . . ." he said, "and I will let your people go to offer sacrifices to the Lord."

"When would you like the frogs to be gone?" asked Moses.

"Tomorrow!" said Pharaoh.

"Very well," said Moses, "it will be as you say, so that you may know there is no one like the Lord our God." He promised that the frogs would leave the palace and the people's houses the next day. The only frogs left would be "those that remain in the Nile."

108

FROGS IN THE PALACE

In the morning, the frogs were all dead. The "frogs died in the houses, in the courtyards and in the fields. They were piled into heaps, and the land reeked of them." I'm sure it did.

But when Pharaoh saw—and smelled—the dead frogs and knew that the plague was over, he changed his mind and refused to keep his part of the bargain. The Bible says "he hardened his heart," which is a bad thing for anybody to do and always leads to trouble.

And more trouble was on the way for Pharaoh.

"Stretch out your staff and strike the dust of the ground," God said to Aaron, "and throughout the land of Egypt the dust will become gnats."

Aaron did, and "gnats came upon men and animals. All the dust throughout the land of Egypt became gnats." There were gnats in the palace—on Pharaoh's servants, on his wife, on his children, and on himself. His magicians, also tormented with gnats, tried to imitate what Moses had done, but failed. "This is the finger of God," they said.

But though these men were beginning to see that there was a power at work in Egypt far greater than any they had ever known, Pharaoh remained as stubborn as ever. Again he hardened his heart.

The next time Moses and Aaron met him, they brought more bad news. If he would not let the children of Israel go, they told him, then God would send swarms of flies, and "the houses of the Egyptians will be full of flies."

109

This time, however, there would be a difference between Egypt and the land of Goshen, where the Hebrews lived. God would allow no flies in Goshen.

"This miraculous sign will occur tomorrow," said Aaron. In the morning the flies appeared. Millions of flies. They buzzed into the people's eyes, into their clothes, into their food. There was no use killing them, for more and still more came, until everyone was frantic.

The palace crawled with as many flies as the home of the humblest Egyptian. Throne room, banqueting hall, and bedrooms were black with flies. At last Pharaoh could stand it no longer. He sent for Moses and Aaron. "Go," he said, "sacrifice to your God here in the land."

Finally he was willing for the Hebrews to take time off for their sacrifice, but it must be done in the land of Egypt.

Moses would not agree. "No," he said, "we want to go to the desert."

"All right," said Pharaoh, driven to desperation, "go if you must. Anything, so long as you get rid of these flies. Just don't go very far away."

Moses promised to ask God to remove the flies, but as soon as he and Aaron were gone, Pharaoh hardened his heart again "and would not let the people go."

Moses and Aaron must have wondered what else would have to happen before this stubborn man would bow to God's will. They did not have long to wait.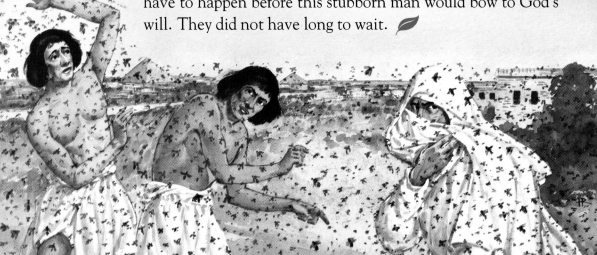

Three Dark Days

(Exodus 9:1-11:8)

I T IS surprising how many times some people have to be punished before they learn to do right.

You would think that after Pharaoh had seen all the water in Egypt turned to blood, after frogs had jumped all over his palace, and after swarms of gnats and flies had tormented him nearly to death, he would finally have learned something. He should have recognized that Moses and Aaron's God, who had sent these dreadful plagues, was not to be taken lightly. But as soon as each plague ended, he hardened his heart again. So he had to suffer some more.

Soon the cattle of Egypt began to die in large numbers— thousands of them. Then painful sores broke out on the people. Even Pharaoh suffered from them. So did his magicians and all his servants.

Next, a wild storm swept down on the country. Never before had Egypt seen such thunder, lightning, and hail. The hail broke down the trees and flattened the entire crop of flax and barley. Then millions of locusts swarmed in and ate every

111

green thing that remained after the storm. The whole country must have looked like a desert.

This meant ruin and starvation for every Egyptian family. It meant ruin for the government too, because no one would have income to be taxed. And while everybody was wondering what dreadful thing would happen next, a great darkness covered the land. The Bible says it was so dark that people couldn't see each other. For three days people did not leave their houses.

Everybody was frightened now, even Pharaoh himself. There was no sunshine during the day; no moonlight at night. Even the stars were blacked out. The darkness was so dense it could be felt. Coming after all the other terrible plagues, it was just too much to bear.

At the end of the third dark day Pharaoh again sent for Moses and Aaron. Just how he found them we are not told. Perhaps two soldiers, holding torches high, felt their way through the darkness to the land of Goshen. To their surprise they saw light shining in the homes of the children of Israel.

Through the thick blackness Moses and Aaron were led to the palace. It must have been an eerie journey, because there wasn't any traffic on the streets—no movement anywhere. Only an awesome silence was felt, broken by the barking of dogs and the cries of terrified children.

"Go!" said Pharaoh angrily as the two men came before him. "Go, serve the Lord!"

This time he was willing for all the Israelites to go—men, women, and children—but not their cattle. Since the cattle of Egypt had been killed, he naturally had his eye on the

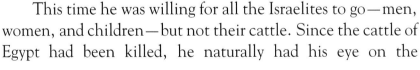

Hebrews' beautiful flocks and herds, which had been spared from the plagues.

But Moses would not agree. The Hebrews would take their cattle with them. They would need them for sacrifices, he said.

Moses' response made Pharaoh angrier than ever.

"Get out!" he cried. "Make sure you do not appear before me again! The day you see my face you will die."

Moses himself was beginning to get annoyed now, and he said something full of meaning that Pharaoh did not understand—not then. "Just as you say," he said, coldly. "I will never appear before you again."

Then, with rising irritation in his voice, Moses told the king that one last terrible plague was about to fall upon him and his people. "This is what the Lord says: 'About midnight I will go throughout Egypt. Every firstborn son in Egypt will die, from the firstborn son of Pharaoh, who sits on the throne, to the firstborn son of the slave girl, who is at her hand mill, and all the firstborn of the cattle as well. There will be loud wailing throughout Egypt—worse than there has ever been or ever will be again. . . . All these officials of yours will come to me, bowing down before me and saying, "Go, you and all the people who follow you!" After that I will leave.' Then Moses, hot with anger, left Pharaoh."

The darkness had passed now, and as Moses, with Aaron at his side, strode through the streets, the people looked at them in awe. What men had ever been able to work such miracles before? What men had been able to see Pharaoh 10 times in a row and come away alive? The Bible says, "Moses himself was

2-8

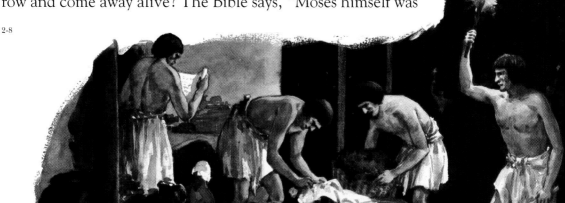

highly regarded in Egypt by Pharaoh's officials and by the people."

Now things began to happen fast. Knowing that only a few hours remained before the great Exodus would begin, Moses told the Hebrews to visit the Egyptians and ask "for articles of silver and gold." These valuables were not really wages, but the Hebrews had worked long years as slaves. Perhaps the Egyptians recognized that they owed the Hebrews something. Anyway, they willingly gave their silver and gold.

Then word was sent from home to home through all the land of Goshen, to every Hebrew family: "This is the night we will be freed. Tonight God will strike down all the firstborn of Egypt. Then Pharaoh will let us go. Pack your things. Prepare food for a long journey. Get ready to leave. Tomorrow we will be on our way to freedom!"

Imagine the excitement everywhere. It all seemed too good to be true. Old men and women, who had labored long years for the Egyptians and had been beaten many times by the slave drivers, cried out with thankful hearts, "Thank God! Thank God! It's over at last! God has kept His promise!"

Boys and girls looked up into their mother's face and asked, "Are we really going away, Mamma? Where are we going? To the land flowing with milk and honey you told us about?"

And when their mother said, "Yes, that's just where we are going," they danced around and shouted happily, "Hooray! Hooray! We're off to the land of Canaan!"

PART THREE

Stories of

the Exodus

(Exodus 11:1-18:27)

Blood on the Doorposts

(Exodus 12:1-36)

O
N THAT last afternoon in Egypt every Hebrew father and mother had a secret worry. If what Moses had said was true, the Lord was coming that night to strike down all the firstborn in the country. Would He make any mistakes? In the darkness and with so many homes to visit, would He be able to tell the difference between an Egyptian home and an Israelite home?

To make sure that His people would not suffer from this last awful plague, God told them to take the blood of a lamb or baby goat and sprinkle it above and on either side of the doorposts to their homes. "And when I see the blood," He said, "I will pass over you."

All who believed that Moses spoke for God obeyed the command. That evening faithful Hebrews all through the land of Goshen killed a perfect little lamb or goat and sprinkled its blood on their doorposts.

Everywhere men and women asked one another, "Is the blood sprinkled on your home?" And if a home didn't have

117

← PAINTING BY ARLO GREER

The night when Israel was to leave Egypt every parent sprinkled the blood of a lamb on the doorposts of his house to show he believed God would save his family from death.

blood by its entrance, neighbors would bang on the door and urge, "Don't forget the blood!"

It must have been quite a sight. I can imagine that each family stood outside its home as the father, holding a basin of blood in one hand and a sprig of hyssop in the other, sprinkled first one doorpost and then the other. In all the families the oldest sons were especially interested in what was happening because they would die if the job was not done properly.

Some people might have said, "Why do we have to sprinkle blood around our door anyway? What good can this do us?" If they did, they soon learned that it was dangerous not to put up God's sign of safety.

Thousands of lambs must have died that last evening Israel spent in Egypt. Every one of them was a symbol of Jesus, "the Lamb of God, who takes away the sin of the world." [1] The blood sprinkled on the doorposts was a symbol of the cleansing blood of Jesus, which was "poured out for many." [2]

Like the Hebrews in Egypt, we need to do just what God asks us to do. When we accept Jesus as our Saviour, it's as if we are sprinkling His blood on the door of our hearts. Then He will forgive our sins, and will pass over us in the day of judgment. This is what the apostle Paul meant when he said, "Christ, our Passover lamb, has been sacrificed." [3]

118

BLOOD ON THE DOORPOSTS

What happened to the lamb whose blood was sprinkled on the doorposts? It was roasted whole and eaten by the entire family. They ate it "in haste," with everyone fully dressed, ready to leave at a moment's notice.

I doubt anyone slept that night. The Egyptians may have, for an hour or two, but not the Hebrews. Fathers and mothers were too busy packing and getting things ready for the long journey ahead of them. And the children were too excited. Everyone must have been eagerly waiting for the signal to leave Egypt. Tired as they all were, this was no night for sleep.

Suddenly a dreadful sound rose on the midnight air. From all over the country of Egypt came the screams of frightened women, mingled with the wailing of thousands of people crying over their dead. The Egyptians, who had killed so many of the Hebrews' children, were learning what it meant to lose their own children.

"At midnight the Lord struck down all the firstborn in Egypt, from the firstborn of Pharaoh, who sat on the throne, to the firstborn of the prisoner, who was in the dungeon, and the firstborn of all the livestock as well."

This was the last and most terrible of all the plagues. Finally Pharaoh was ready to surrender. He didn't have much

left to fight over. The Bible says he "got up during the night, and there was loud wailing in Egypt, for there was not a house without someone dead. During the night Pharaoh summoned Moses and Aaron and said, 'Up! Leave my people, you and the Israelites! Go, worship the Lord as you have requested. Take your flocks and herds, . . . and go.' "

With death in every home in Egypt, the Egyptians did not want to keep the Hebrews any longer. They wanted the Hebrews to go *now*. "The Egyptians urged the people to hurry and leave the country." They even heaped silver and gold and clothing on them, they were so anxious for them to be gone. They gave the Hebrews anything they asked for. The Bible says the Hebrews "plundered the Egyptians."

That was one of the great nights of history. It was a night when a nation was born, a night when thousands of slaves became free, a night to be remembered through all time to come.

And it was on that night that God's promise to Abraham came true. Long ago He had told His faithful servant that after hundreds of years his children would be delivered from Egyptian bondage. Now the time had come, and they were free again. Now they could go back to the homeland they had dreamed of for so many years.

---

[1] John 1:29.
[2] Mark 14:24.
[3] 1 Corinthians 5:7.

On to Freedom!

(Exodus 12:37-42; 13:17-22)

THE SUN rose the next day over a country that was in deep mourning. Death had entered every Egyptian home. Thousands of bodies waited for burial. All the firstborn sons, from the crown prince in the palace to the oldest child of the humblest boatman on the Nile, had died—along with the firstborn of all their animals.

In Goshen, however, every household was busy and excited. Most of the Hebrews had been awake all night. Now, as news spread that Pharaoh had finally agreed to let them go, they were overjoyed. Eagerly they grabbed each other's hands and cried, "We're free, we're free!"

Some of them gloated over the piles of gold and silver ornaments they had collected from the Egyptians. They wondered what they would do with so much wealth. Others thanked God for His protecting care through the night.

But they had no time to waste. Pharaoh might change his mind again, as he had before. If they were going to leave Egypt, they had to go right away.

121

ON TO FREEDOM!

Moses had already told the leaders of Israel where everyone was to gather. Before sunrise thousands of people were looking around their homes for the last time before they headed with their families toward the meeting place. Their wagons, pulled by oxen, were loaded with tents, bedding, pots for cooking, jars of food, bundles of clothing, and other things they wanted to take along.

Some mothers had babies strapped to their backs, and others had bread dough "on their shoulders in kneading troughs wrapped in clothing." If you had been there, you might have seen a little boy with a toy in one hand trying to lead a lamb with his other hand. You might have seen a little girl carrying a doll in one hand and holding her baby sister's hand in the other, for I'm sure little girls had dolls back then just as they do now.

All kinds of people, old and young, grandpas and tiny tots, were in that moving crowd. Mixed up with them were all sorts of animals—cows, bulls, donkeys, sheep, and goats. As Moses watched the people gathering with their flocks and herds, he must have wondered how he would ever get such a large company safely to Canaan.

Now he could put to use his early training in the royal palace. Part of his education as a prince had been in the army, so he knew how to keep large numbers of people in order. Working with the leaders of Israel, he soon had the crowd forming into a line and moving out along the route he planned to take them. Gradually a long procession took shape as the

← PAINTING BY HERBERT RUDEEN

The great day of deliverance from Egyptian slavery had come at last, and there was great excitement. Everyone was eager to start on the journey through the wilderness to Canaan.

Hebrews started out for Canaan.

It must have taken hours just to get everything ready, because there were "about six hundred thousand men on foot, besides women and children" "as well as large droves of livestock, both flocks and herds."

And that wasn't all. Moses soon noticed that many people who were not Hebrews had joined the procession. Some of them might have been Egyptian servants who saw a chance to get away from their masters. Others might have just been looking for adventure. Whoever they were, they insisted on going along—and what a lot of trouble they caused later on! Moses must have wished many times that he had stopped them right at the beginning.

At last the great caravan was on its way. Slowly, ever so slowly, it inched forward, gradually leaving behind Rameses and other cities that the Hebrews had helped build. The pyramids grew smaller and smaller until they were nothing more than mere specks on the horizon.

The teenagers and children probably wished they could move faster, but it was impossible. There were so many

babies—and sheep and goats and calves—that they couldn't be hurried. Some of the men must have had a great deal of trouble trying to keep the flocks and herds moving at all. Often a cow or sheep would wander off and have to be chased back into line.

Somewhere in the procession was something that created quite a bit of excitement. It was a coffin. Among all his preparations for the Exodus, Moses had not forgotten Joseph's request that his bones be taken to Canaan.

At first nobody felt tired. Not even the children. They were all so happy and excited to be leaving Egypt that they forgot how weary they really were. They had been so busy getting ready for the journey and finding their right place in the procession that they hadn't had time to think that they were homeless now, without a place to sleep at night. They had been too busy to worry about the future or how they would get food and water.

They had just wanted to put as many miles as possible between themselves and Pharaoh, in case he changed his mind and came after them. But as it grew later in the day and the children got tired and hungry, the fathers and mothers began to

wonder about some of these things. How long would the journey take? When would they be able to settle down in their new homes in Canaan? Had they brought along enough food for everybody? What about water? Would they meet any enemies along the way? Would wild animals in the desert attack them?

Suddenly a shout seemed to echo down the long line of people. "The cloud! Look at the cloud!"

All day they had been enveloped in clouds of dust kicked up by the herds of cattle, but this was different. It looked more like a pillar of cloud that went straight up ahead of the procession.

"See the cloud, Mamma!" cried the boys and girls. "See the cloud!"

"I see it!" said a thousand worried mothers. "But what is it? What does it mean?"

Then word passed down the line from Moses that God was in the cloud and would lead His people all the way they had to go. As the sun set and the sky grew dark, the cloud glowed with a light so beautiful that the people called it a pillar of fire. It was comforting to know—that first night away from home—that God was so near.

No one needed to worry about the future anymore. Since the great God of Abraham, Isaac, and Jacob was leading them, everything would be all right. He would take care of everything. He would bring them into Canaan safe and sound.

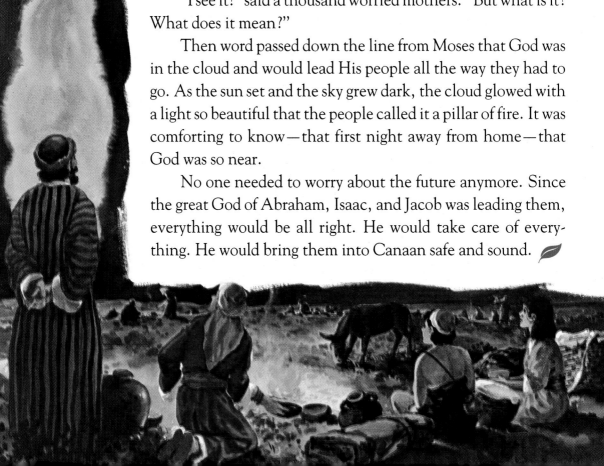

Walking Through the Sea

(Exodus 13:17-22; 14:1-22)

EARLY the next morning, even before the sun rose, the Hebrews were up and busy. They all wanted to get on their way as soon as they could. Quickly the animals were fed and the children given their breakfast. Then, as the pillar of cloud moved slowly forward, those in front followed it, and the caravan moved on.

Of course they all expected to go straight to Canaan, a journey that would have taken them only a few weeks at the most. But when they reached a little place called Etham, less than 150 miles (240 kilometers) from the border of Canaan, Moses ordered them to turn south and go "around by the desert road toward the Red Sea."

Everyone was surprised, and many said, "This isn't the way to Canaan!"

But God had a reason for leading His people this direction. If they had taken the direct route to Canaan, they would have had to pass through the land of the Philistines, who would have fought them. God knew that if these poor people just out of

127

slavery would have to fight, they would lose courage and run back to Egypt.

So on they went in the wrong direction—at least it seemed like the wrong direction. You can imagine how the people watched the pillar of cloud all day to see whether it would turn back and go where they thought it should go. But it didn't turn. It moved slowly forward till it came to a place called Pi Hahiroth, on the shores of the Red Sea. Here Moses told the people to make camp for the night.

The men and women must have talked about this strange turn of events as they prepared the evening meal. I can almost hear someone saying, "Seems to me we're going to Ethiopia, not Canaan." And another saying, "Nice place to get caught if the Egyptians come after us! We have mountains on one side and the Red Sea on the other."

Little boys must have asked, "Daddy, are we going to sail over the sea in boats? Where are the boats?"

Suddenly a man pointed back along the way they had just come and cried in alarm. Far in the distance a cloud of dust was rising. In the middle of it were moving figures. Soldiers! Chariots! The Egyptians!

It was just what the Hebrews had feared most. Pharaoh had changed his mind. Not only did he want revenge for the death of his son and so many of his subjects, but he wanted his slaves back. He had forgotten the plagues, and he was determined to get back the cattle and the gold and silver jewelry the Hebrews had taken.

You see, when Pharaoh learned that the Hebrews had left,

128

taking all their cattle with them, he couldn't believe it at first. But when he realized they had really gone, he shouted, " 'What have we done? We have let the Israelites go and have lost their services!'

"So he had his chariot made ready and took his army with him. He took six hundred of the best chariots, along with all the other chariots of Egypt. . . . He pursued the Israelites. . . . The Egyptians . . . overtook them as they camped by the sea."

As the Hebrews saw the chariots rushing toward them they grew terrified. They knew how cruel the Egyptians could be. They knew what would happen if the Egyptians reached them with their whips and swords and spears. They rushed to Moses and almost shrieked at him in their fear, "Why did you bring us out here to die in this desert?"

It was a dark hour for Moses. He, too, had seen the Egyptians coming, and he knew just what they would do to him if they caught him. But he was sure that God had not brought His people this far to let them be killed by the Egyptians. Moses had not forgotten the great miracles God had worked during the past few weeks, and he was certain that God would work another miracle now, if necessary.

"Do not be afraid!" he cried bravely to the people. "Stand firm and you will see the deliverance the Lord will bring you today. The Egyptians you see today you will never see again. The Lord will fight for you; you need only to be still."

Even as Moses spoke, something began to happen. The pillar of cloud moved mysteriously toward the onrushing Egyp-

2-9

tians. It became a barrier between them and the frightened Hebrews. As night fell, the cloud brought dense darkness to the Egyptians but glowed with warmth and cheer on the camp of Israel.

Moses prayed to God, telling Him all that had happened. But this was not only a time for prayer, but for action. "Why are you crying out to me?" God asked him. "Tell the Israelites to move on. Raise your staff and stretch out your hand over the sea to divide the water so that the Israelites can go through the sea on dry ground."

Suddenly the wind began to blow. And what a wind! It roared in from the east, throwing up huge clouds of sand in the desert and lashing the Red Sea into a foaming mass of whitecapped waves.

WALKING THROUGH THE SEA

Standing on the shore, his staff in his outstretched hand, Moses watched the tremendous sight. This was no ordinary storm. God was working through the wind. He was cutting a path through the sea!

Down, down, went the water until the sea bottom was uncovered! Straight ahead, from shore to shore, was a wide strip of solid land.

"Forward!" cried the leaders of Israel, passing on the word of command. "Forward! Everybody forward!"

I wonder who went first. It took courage, a lot of courage, with those towering walls of water on either side. What a pity we don't know! Perhaps it was a little boy, leading his pet goat. Perhaps it was a brave little girl, anxious to save her baby sister. I don't know. But *somebody* was first to step onto that strange, windswept avenue through the stormy sea.

Now another plucked up courage to go, and another, and another, while thousands lined the shore and waited for their turn.

"Hurry! Hurry!" everyone was saying. Nobody knew when the wind would stop blowing. Nobody knew when the water would come crashing down again. Nobody knew when Pharaoh would discover what was going on and dash after them.

Now there were hundreds of people half walking, half running, along this path through the sea. The cows, donkeys, goats, and sheep were moving forward with them as fast as they could, and getting in everybody's way.

It was a marvelous, never-to-be-forgotten sight. Moses stood tirelessly with his staff stretched out over the sea, his long white beard blowing this way and that by the raging wind. The dark green barricades of water, with foam and spray whirling up from their tossing summits, rose on either side of the anxious crowds as they rushed on to safety. A worried old man whacked a stubborn donkey, a frightened mother dragged her scared children, and two careless boys threw stones at the walls of water. And this whole amazing scene was lighted up by the bright glow from the pillar of fire.

Could Israel ever forget this night?

Song of Victory

(Exodus 14:21-15:21)

HOUR after hour the strange procession continued, as men, women, and children fled for dear life along the corridor God had made through the sea. Drivers of wagons shouted at their oxen, urging them to move faster. Shepherds frantically drove their herds of cattle and the flocks of sheep and goats as they tried to make them run to the other shore. Mothers begged their little ones not to lag behind.

Ahead was the one hope of safety. Behind were the Egyptians, scarcely a mile (1.6 kilometers) away. Who could tell when they would discover that everyone was escaping? And who could tell how long the water would remain piled up on either side, "congealed in the heart of the sea," as the Bible says it was?

On, on, on, they hurried—thousands of men, women, and children dashing pell-mell for the other shore. How long it took for so many to make the crossing, we are not told. Finally,

133

however, the last wagon had been helped up the opposite bank. The last father and mother had scrambled onto higher ground. The last shepherd had driven the last sheep out of the danger zone, and the last lost little boys and girls were safe with their parents again.

What a sigh of relief went up from everyone as they looked back and saw that the channel was clear! Everyone had reached the other shore! No one was left behind!

But what was that moving onto the shore they had just left? Spears! Swords! Chariots! The Egyptians! They were rushing down the opposite bank! They were marching right through the channel between the walls of water!

"O God!" cried the people in their fear and anguish. "O God, help us! Save us from the Egyptians!"

That first chariot stopped! Its wheels had sunk into mud. The driver was whipping his horses, trying to get them to pull the chariot out, but it wouldn't move.

Now another chariot bogged down, and another. Their wheels had come off! The confusion grew worse and worse. Other chariots, trying to pass those in front, got all tangled up with the ones that had broken down. Angry shouts rose above the shrieking of the wind.

"Look out! Can't you see where you're going?"

"Go on, go on!" cried the officers. But they couldn't go on. The path through the sea was not passable.

"Go back! Go back!" someone yelled.

But it was too late. They couldn't go back. There was no room to turn round. They were trapped.

"During the last watch of the night," the Bible says, "the Lord looked down from the pillar of fire and cloud at the Egyptian army and threw it into confusion. He made the wheels of their chariots

come off so that they had difficulty driving. And the Egyptians said, 'Let's get away from the Israelites! The Lord is fighting for them against Egypt.' "

Everyone looked at Moses. He was standing erect, looking bravely—defiantly—at the oncoming army of Pharaoh. His staff was stretched out once more over the windswept water.

As Moses held his staff above the sea, the wind changed. At God's command it had cut this amazing path through the sea and had kept it open while Israel passed to safety. Now the wind brought the walls of water tumbling down, covering the chariots and drowning the soldiers.

"The water flowed back and covered the chariots and horsemen—the entire army of Pharaoh that had followed the Israelites into the sea. Not one of them survived."

At sunrise the wind died, and the sea became calm again. It was hard to believe that such a wonderful thing could have happened in this desert place. The distant mountains, the sandy beaches, the blue ribbon of water, were just the same as they had been before. Nothing remained to remind Israel of God's great miracle except the bodies of the Egyptians washed up on the shore.

But these corpses told a story that brought peace to every heart. For the first time in their lives, the Hebrews did not have to worry about the Egyptians. Now that Egypt had been ruined by the 10 terrible plagues and Pharaoh's best troops had been drowned, the Israelites could forget the past and turn their faces bravely toward the future that God was planning for them.

Now someone was singing. Above the buzz of talking, the lowing of cattle, and the bleating of sheep, came a rich, deep voice in a song of praise to God. It was Moses! And what a song! Soon all joined in, singing from their hearts.

"I will sing to the Lord, for he is highly exalted. The horse and its rider he has hurled into the sea. The Lord is my strength and my song; he has become my salvation. He is my God, . . . my father's God, and I will exalt him. But you blew with your breath, and the sea covered them. They sank like lead in the mighty waters. Who among the gods is like you, O Lord? Who is like you—majestic in holiness,

awesome in glory, working wonders?"

The men paused, then the women began to sing, led by Miriam, Aaron's and Moses' sister. She had been the one who had watched over Moses long ago, when he had been a baby in that basket among the bulrushes. She held a hand drum that she played as all the women took up the chorus, "Sing to the Lord, for he is highly exalted. The horse and its rider he has hurled into the sea."

Everybody was so happy, happy beyond words. Their old, ugly life in Egypt was gone forever. Their days of slavery were over. They were free! They were safe from their enemies! And they would gladly have stayed right there by the Red Sea and kept on singing forever.

But Moses knew better. They had a long way to go. They must move on. So when the song of praise ended, he gave orders for the caravan to get ready to start once more on its journey.

Food in the Desert

(Exodus 15:22-27; 16:1-36)

FOR THREE long, hot days the great caravan moved on through the desert. People began to get tired and thirsty. The water they had brought along with them was almost gone. When children asked their parents for a drink, they were told they couldn't have one. Those in charge of the cattle began to get worried about what would happen to the animals if they couldn't find water soon.

Thousands of men, women, and children can drink a lot of water on a hot day. So can thousands of cows, sheep, and goats. If they couldn't find water, they couldn't go on.

By the end of the third day many of the marchers were beginning to get worried. But then someone who was scouting far ahead began to wave excitedly. "Water!" he cried. "Water!"

Just hearing the word *water* made everyone feel better. Fathers, mothers, and children began to smile, and they pushed on eagerly. But when the first people to reach the pool stooped down to drink the water, they were terribly disappointed. It was so bitter that it wasn't fit to drink.

Quickly the word sped back along the line. "The water's bad. We cannot drink it." They called the place Marah, or "bitterness."

The people began to grumble and blame Moses. Why had he brought them to such a spot? Didn't he know they would need water? They must have thought that Moses, who had lived in the desert for 40 years, didn't know about the water problem!

"What are we to drink?" they cried.

As always, Moses took his troubles to God, and God had a way out. He pointed to a certain tree, which he told Moses to cut down and throw into the bitter water. When Moses did this, the water became sweet and drinkable.

"Then they came to Elim, where there were twelve springs and seventy palm trees, and they camped there near the water." Everybody was happy now. This was the first real rest they had had since leaving Egypt. After all the excitement, the lack of sleep, and the long march, they were just about worn out. They

were very glad for Elim, with its cool, fresh water and its palm trees.

The Israelites camped here for two or three weeks, and then Moses ordered them to pack their tents and start on their way again. So "on the fifteenth day of the second month," just six weeks after leaving Egypt, they came into the Desert of Sin—a dry, rocky country, with little pasture for the cattle and no place to grow food.

"What a place!" muttered some. "Why has he brought us here?"

"If we'd gone north instead of south, we would have been in Canaan by now," said others.

"What does he think we're going to grow here?" asked a farmer, comparing the dry sand with the rich soil of the Nile valley.

"And how does he think we're going to keep our cattle alive on this poor scrubland?" asked another.

Their complaints were catching, and soon everyone was grumbling. As food supplies got lower and lower, the whole community turned on Moses and Aaron like they always did when they were in trouble.

Forgetting all the miracles God had worked for them in Egypt, at the Red Sea, and at Marah, they cried out, "If only we had died by the Lord's hand in Egypt! There we sat around pots of meat and ate all the food we wanted, but you have brought us

141

out into this desert to starve this entire assembly to death."

It was a silly thing to say, but they had been slaves so long they didn't know any better. Even though they had seen God do many wonderful things for them, they still didn't understand Him or trust Him. They just wanted to have enough to eat. They thought they would be willing to be slaves again if they could only smell the meat they used to have.

Moses told God what the people were saying and asked Him what to do. God promised that He would "rain down bread from heaven."

That evening, just as the people were wondering what to eat for supper, thousands of birds flew into the camp. They were quails, and they flew so low that it was easy to kill them. Everyone had a good meal, and some must have remembered to thank God for looking after them once more.

But what about breakfast? There were no stores where they could buy shredded wheat or corn flakes. What sort of food would God provide in the morning? many wondered. Would He send quails again? No. Instead, He sent something quite different.

142

Early the next day, as soon as the dew had gone, "thin flakes like frost on the ground appeared on the desert floor. When the Israelites saw it, they said to each other, 'What is it?' For they did not know what it was. Moses said to them, 'It is the bread the Lord has given you to eat.' " The people called it "manna." In the Hebrew language "manna" means "What is it?"

They picked up the first little piece and tasted it cautiously, but it was nice! It had a sweet taste "like wafers made with honey." They liked it. How all those poor, hungry people, especially the boys and girls, enjoyed that delicious breakfast!

Morning after morning, they found the "What is it?" bread, or "manna," right at their tent doors. All they had to do was gather it and eat it. For the next 40 years, this was their main source of food.

But there was something strange about the manna. It appeared on the ground only six days a week, but never on the seventh day—not one little tiny piece.

Why? Because God wanted to teach His people to keep His Sabbath holy. Adam and Eve had kept the Sabbath in the beginning of the world. So had Abraham, Isaac, and Jacob. When the children of Israel went into Egypt, at Joseph's invitation, they had kept it too; but when they had been made slaves, they had not been able to keep it. During that time, many began to think that it didn't matter, that God didn't expect them to keep it anymore. Some had even forgotten which day was the Sabbath.

143

FOOD IN THE DESERT

So now, by the miracle of the manna, God tried to bring His people back into the right and true way. Every Friday they gathered double the amount of manna they usually collected, so they would have enough to last over the Sabbath.

The manna gathered on Friday kept for two days, but any manna left over on any of the other days quickly spoiled. This, plus the fact that no manna appeared on the seventh day, let the people see which day God wanted them to keep as the Sabbath. There simply couldn't be any doubt about it. It was the seventh day, and no other day would do.

At first some people didn't believe that God meant what He said. These people went out to pick up manna on the seventh day, but they couldn't find any. God was displeased and said, "How long will you refuse to keep my commands and my instructions? Bear in mind that the Lord has given you the Sabbath; that is why on the sixth day he gives you bread for two days. Everyone is to stay where he is on the seventh day; no one is to go out."

This lesson, taught once a week for 40 years, fixed in the minds of the Israelites the right day on which to keep the Sabbath. God said to them 2,080 times (52 multiplied by 40), "This day, the seventh day, is My Sabbath." He didn't want them ever to forget it or to have any excuse for making a mistake about it.

They never did forget it. Even now—more than 3,000 years later—they have not forgotten it. How could they? How could anybody? ✐

← PAINTING BY RUSSELL HARLAN

Food was not easy to find in the wilderness, so God sent manna from heaven every day. But on the sixth day of the week He sent a double portion, to last them over the Sabbath.

Too Busy Doing Good

(Exodus 17:1-18:26)

NO LONGER worried about food, Israel traveled on down the peninsula of Sinai. Then the water problem came up again. By the time they reached Rephidim, they had no water left.

As usual, they blamed Moses. "Give us water to drink!" they cried. "Why did you bring us up out of Egypt to make us and our children and livestock die of thirst?" Some even asked, "Is the Lord among us or not?"

They were so angry that Moses cried out to God, "What am I to do with these people? They are almost ready to stone me."

God told Moses to take some of the leading men in the camp to a certain rock in Horeb. He was to strike this rock with his staff, and water would flow from it.

The group of leaders went with Moses and saw him strike the rock. Water gushed out of it, more than enough to take care

of the needs of the people and the cattle.

Hardly was this problem solved, however, when more trouble came—this from the people of Amalek, who did not like having the Israelites passing through their country. Maybe they thought this was a good chance to steal some of the Israelites' cattle. Anyhow, their soldiers swooped down out of the mountains one day and caught Israel by surprise.

A young man named Joshua led the men of Israel into battle. With Aaron and Hur, Moses watched the fight from a hilltop. After some time these two men noticed that when Moses held up his hands, the soldiers of Israel advanced. When Moses dropped his hands, Amalek's soldiers began to win. So Aaron and Hur found a stone for Moses to sit on, and they held up his hands, "one on one side, one on the other," until Israel won the victory.

By sunset the Amalekites were running away, and Moses was able to rest his weary arms. Then he built an altar to the Lord, calling it Jehovah-nissi, which means "the Lord is my banner." The soldiers understood why. They had seen him holding up his hands in prayer to God for them all day—just as though he had been holding up a banner to inspire them to do their best.

From Rephidim, Israel journeyed to the Wilderness of Sinai, and camped near "the mountain of God." Soon after this, word reached Moses that Jethro, his father-in-law, was coming to see him. He was bringing Zipporah, Moses' wife, and his two sons, Gershom and Eliezer.

Moses went out to meet Jethro and his family. He bowed respectfully to his father-in-law and kissed him. Then they all gathered together in Moses' tent to talk over all that had happened since Moses had left Midian to go to Egypt.

I imagine those two boys were glad to see their father again, don't you? And how surprised they must have been to see so many people! Having lived in the country all their lives, looking after their grandfather's sheep, they had never dreamed there were so many men, women, and children in all the world!

They had so much to talk about! "Moses told his father-in-law about everything the Lord had done to Pharaoh and the Egyptians for Israel's sake and about all the hardships they had met along the way and how the Lord had saved them.

"Jethro was delighted to hear about all the good things the Lord had done for Israel." "Now I know," he said, "that the Lord is greater than all other gods."

Then Jethro had a special meal for Moses. He invited Aaron and all the elders of Israel to welcome his guest.

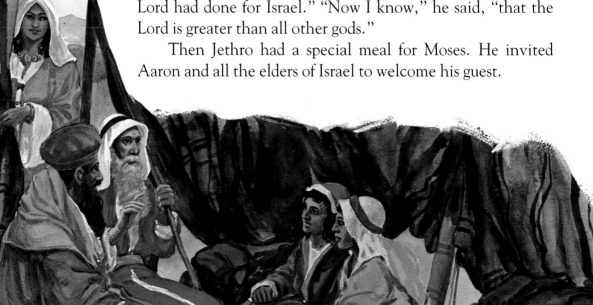

The next morning "Moses took his seat to serve as judge for the people, and they stood around him from morning till evening."

The people needed advice on so many things and there were so many cases of misunderstanding between one person and another that Moses was kept talking and answering questions all day long.

Jethro stood by, watching and listening. When he was able to speak to Moses alone, he gave him some good advice. "You can't stand this," he said. "You'll wear yourself out."

"But the people keep coming to me," Moses said, "and I have to judge between them and inform them of God's decrees and laws."

"It's too much for you," said Jethro. "You can't do all this by yourself."

He suggested that Moses divide the work and let some of the other men help him. "Select capable men from all the people," Jethro said, "—men who fear God, trustworthy men who hate dishonest gain—and appoint them as officials over thousands, hundreds, fifties and tens. Have *them* serve as judges for the people at all times, but have them bring every difficult case to you; the simple cases they can decide themselves. That will make your load lighter, because they will share it with you."

It was good advice. Moses, with the best intentions in the world, was trying to do too much. He was actually too busy doing good. He liked to be the father of his people, meeting all their needs and answering all their questions, but no one could do all this and keep well. As Jethro said, he was just wearing himself out, and he would die long before his work was done.

Fortunately, Moses was humble enough to take advice—which is more than some boys and girls I know will do. He followed Jethro's suggestion and "chose capable men from all Israel and made them leaders of the people, officials over thousands, hundreds, fifties and tens. They served as judges for the people at all times. The difficult cases they brought to Moses, but the simple ones they decided themselves."

It was a good thing that Moses did as he was told, for big events were about to happen. In just a little while he would have to spend 40 days and 40 nights with God on Mount Sinai. If he hadn't given up most of his work as judge and counselor of the people, he would never have been able to do the far greater things God wanted him to do.

He would have been too busy to seize life's greatest opportunities, too busy to receive the tablets of the law from its holy Author, too busy to meet God face-to-face.

It pays to take advice from a good person.

PART FOUR

Stories of

Moses *and* the Tabernacle

(Exodus 19:1 to Leviticus 8:36)

Ten Golden Rules

(Exodus 19; 20:1-17; 31:18)

THREE months after the children of Israel had been delivered from Egyptian slavery, they still hadn't reached Canaan. They were camped in a very hot desert in the shadow of Mount Sinai. Instead of going north, the pillar of cloud had moved south. Here they were, hundreds of miles from where they had expected to be at this time.

Why had God done this?

He had some lessons He wanted to teach His people. He needed time and a private place, shut off from the rest of the world, to instruct them. Since He was planning a great future for these people, God wanted to have them all to Himself for a while until He was sure they understood what sort of people He wanted them to be and what kind of work He wanted them to do.

God had not brought the Israelites out of Egypt with such wonderful miracles just so they could be like other nations. He wanted them to be completely different.

153

← PAINTING BY RUSSELL HARLAN

The first four commandments of the Decalogue teach us our duty to God, and the last six our duty to men. This wonderful law given to Israel through Moses has never been changed.

Eve's Offspring Jesus, who would crush the snake's head, would be born to one of their descendants. God wanted them to be His chief helpers in telling all people about His plan of salvation. They were to tell the story of His love for this world—how He had created it in the beginning and how He plans to restore it to its Edenic beauty someday.

If these people were to be His witnesses, telling others about their holy God, they needed to be holy also. They needed to know right from wrong. They needed always to gladly choose the right. They needed to know why sin is hateful—and to hate it themselves.

But how could they be a holy people when they knew so little about what God expected of them? True, some knowledge of His laws and standards had come down to them through Abraham, Isaac, Jacob, Joseph, and their own parents. However, during their long, sad years as slaves in Egypt, they had lived and worked among idolaters, forgetting many of God's teachings.

God knew all this, so He decided to explain just what He wanted His people to do. He would give His instructions so clearly that through all time to come no one could be mistaken about them or misunderstand them.

God decided that He would talk to His people from Mount Sinai, but first He told Moses to prepare the people for this special occasion. They were to take two days to clean up and

wash their clothes. "Be ready by the third day," Moses told them, "because on that day the Lord will come down on Mount Sinai in the sight of all the people." This was to be a very solemn, wonderful experience that they would never forget for the rest of their lives.

Great excitement filled the camp. The mighty God who had saved them from the Egyptians, who had cut a path through the Red Sea, and who had sent them bread from heaven and water from the rock, was coming near. The wonderful God they had talked and dreamed about from childhood was going to speak to them.

The days of preparation quickly passed. On the morning of the third day, Mount Sinai became like a volcano. Its summit was wrapped in a fiery cloud. "There was thunder and lightning, with a thick cloud over the mountain. . . . Mount Sinai was covered with smoke, because the Lord descended on it in fire. The smoke billowed up from it like smoke from a furnace, the whole mountain trembled violently."

It was an awesome sight, and the children of Israel shook with fear. Even the boys and girls stood silent and still as they gazed in wide-eyed wonder at the mighty spectacle.

Suddenly, from far up on the mountain, out of the middle of the fire and the smoke, came a deep, rich, melodious voice. God's voice!

"And God spoke all these words: 'I am the Lord your God, who brought you out of Egypt, out of the land of slavery.' "

155

Then He declared His holy will in the Ten Commandments:

1. "You shall have no other gods before me."

2. "You shall not make for yourself an idol in the form of anything in heaven above or on the earth beneath or in the waters below. You shall not bow down to them or worship them; for I, the Lord your God, am a jealous God, punishing the children for the sin of the fathers to the third and fourth generation of those who hate me, but showing love to a thousand generations of those who love me and keep my commandments."

3. "You shall not misuse the name of the Lord your God, for the Lord will not hold anyone guiltless who misuses his name."

4. "Remember the Sabbath day by keeping it holy. Six days you shall labor and do all your work, but the seventh day is a Sabbath to the Lord your God. On it you shall not do any work, neither you, nor your son or daughter, nor your manservant or maidservant, nor your animals, nor the alien within your gates. For in six days the Lord made the heavens and the earth, the sea, and all that is in them, but he rested on the

156

seventh day. Therefore the Lord blessed the Sabbath day and made it holy.''

5. "Honor your father and your mother, so that you may live long in the land the Lord your God is giving you.''

6. "You shall not murder.''

7. "You shall not commit adultery.''

8. "You shall not steal.''

9. "You shall not give false testimony against your neighbor.''

10. "You shall not covet your neighbor's house. You shall not covet your neighbor's wife, or his manservant or maidservant, his ox or donkey, or anything that belongs to your neighbor.''

As the people listened to that lovely voice speaking with such majesty and power, but with a tenderness they had never heard before, their hearts were touched. They wanted to obey. They wanted to be good. If this was God's will, then they wanted to do it. So "the people all responded together, 'Everything the Lord has said we will do.' '' They repeated this three times, and I believe they meant it.

But God knew that soon they would forget and that some would begin to question what He had said. Since these commandments were His will for everyone, not just the Israelites, and to show that they are unchangeable, He wrote them on two slabs of stone. The Bible says that "when the Lord finished speaking to Moses on Mount Sinai, he gave him the two tablets of the Testimony, the tablets of stone inscribed by the finger of God.''

God wrote them Himself, with His own finger! How very important they must be!

Jesus thought so too. Long after that wonderful scene, when our loving Saviour came to teach us how to live and show us what God wants, He said, "Until heaven and earth disappear, not the smallest letter, not the least stroke of a pen, will by any means disappear from the Law until everything is accomplished." [1]

And He added these solemn words: "Anyone who breaks one of the least of these commandments and teaches others to do the same will be called least in the kingdom of heaven, but whoever practices and teaches these commands will be called great in the kingdom of heaven." [2]

Even today God wants us to obey these 10 golden rules. All who love Him will want to keep them with His help. They will say with gladness, as the Israelites did long ago, "We will do everything the Lord has said; we will obey."

---

[1] Matthew 5:18.
[2] Matthew 5:19.

Israel's "Traffic" Laws

(Exodus 20:21-26; 21; 22; 23; 24)

AFTER God had spoken from Sinai, telling the children of Israel His 10 golden rules of life, He gave them many other laws that would help them live together peacefully.

Today we have traffic laws that tell us how fast we may drive, what to do when a school bus stops, and how far to stay behind a fire engine. These rules help keep us moving safely and efficiently on the highway. The laws that God gave Israel were designed to help His people understand how to handle problems that arose in the camp.

Unlike God's Ten Commandments, which never change and apply to everybody in all the world, Israel's "traffic" laws do not. They are mostly out of date. But they were very important at the time, for these people had been slaves for many, many years. They didn't know how to behave as free men and women. Some of them even thought slavery was all right. They didn't know any better.

God had to educate them, and so through Moses He taught

159

them first one lesson and then another. He couldn't change their thinking all at once, so He did it little by little.

For instance, knowing that some of the people thought having slaves was all right, He gave orders about how slavery should be regulated. If anyone bought a slave, after six years of service the slave was to be released without having to pay anything. That was a start, at least, toward greater freedom.

And God gave other interesting rules.

If two men got into a fight and one man hurt the other so badly that he had to go to bed, then the one who struck the blow had to help the wounded man get well. He also had to pay the injured man for lost time at work. That was very fair and must have prevented quite a number of fights.

If a man dug a hole and forgot to put a cover on it, and another man's ox or donkey fell into it and was killed, then the man who dug the pit had to pay the other man for the dead animal. This also was fair, don't you think?

If a man allowed his cattle or sheep to graze in a neighbor's field, then he had to pay back his neighbor by giving him

the best hay from his own field.

If one man's ox hurt another man's ox so badly that it died, then the live ox had to be sold and the money divided between the two men. The dead ox was also divided—and so both parties were satisfied.

God told the Israelites that they should never take a bribe. A bribe, He said, makes people lie. How true!

"You must not mistreat a foreigner," was another very fine law, and the reason God gave it was "you know how it feels to be a foreigner. You were foreigners in Egypt" (ICB).

Day after day Moses tried to teach the people all these lessons God had given him on how to behave. They had many questions. Some asked him, "What shall we do in this case, and what shall we do in that?" Through the leaders of thousands, and hundreds, and fifties, and tens, he tried to answer them and show them the right way.

Not everyone, I suppose, liked what he told them. Some wanted to do things the same way they had done them before. Maybe these people asked each other, "Why should we bother about what *he* says?"

The leaders tried their best to enforce the new laws. Gradually the people came to understand that God's way was best, but it must have been a struggle.

One day Moses called the leaders together and told them that God had asked him to come up onto the mountain again and bring Joshua with him. "Wait here for us," Moses said, "until we come back to you. Aaron and Hur are with you, and anyone involved in a dispute can go to them." Then Moses and Joshua waved to the leaders and climbed slowly up toward the summit of Sinai.

"And the glory of the Lord settled on Mount Sinai. . . . To the Israelites the glory of the Lord looked like a consuming fire on top of the mountain. Then Moses entered the cloud."

As Moses and Joshua disappeared, Aaron and the others who were with him turned back toward the camp, wondering how long their leader would be away and what might happen to him up there with God. He had said he would return. But would he?

How could any human being live in the middle of that consuming fire? What if Moses never came back? What would happen to all the people? How could they find their way to Canaan without him?

Before long others began to ask the same questions. As day after day went by and there was no sign of Moses, everyone became more and more worried about him. One week . . . two weeks . . . three weeks passed, and still there was no word out of the cloud.

"He must be dead," the people in the camp said. "We had better return to Egypt."

Moses on the Mount

(Exodus 24:18-32:19)

M OSES stayed on the top of Mount Sinai "forty days and forty nights," almost six weeks.

What was he doing all that time? Something very important. He was listening to God tell a wonderful story.

God told Moses that He planned to live with the Israelites and wanted them to set up a tent-house for Him. "Have them make a sanctuary for me," He said, "and I will dwell among them."

God didn't want them to build a great palace or a massive temple there in the desert. He just wanted a tent or "tabernacle." But every part of it was to be made with perfect care, and it was to mean something special and teach a beautiful lesson.

That's why Moses stayed so long on the mountain. God was so concerned that His tabernacle should be made just right that He told Moses every little detail of what he should do. And Moses must have written it all down so he wouldn't forget anything God had said.

The building was to be something like God's dwelling place in heaven. Of course, God didn't expect Moses to make anything so magnificent and glorious as that. He couldn't have done it, however hard he tried. But he was to follow the same general plan. "See," said God, "that you make them according to the pattern shown you on the mountain."

Of course, God didn't need a place to live on earth. But in the sanctuary God could teach them lessons they needed to learn. There He would try to help them understand how much He loved them and how great a sacrifice He was prepared to make for their salvation. He would help them see how much He hates sin and how they could get rid of it and become the godly people He wanted them to be.

The sanctuary, or tabernacle, was to be portable. It had to be carried from place to place as the children of Israel moved on their way to Canaan. The sides were to be of wood, covered with gold leaf. The roof was to be of four different coverings. The inner one was made of fine linen dyed blue, purple, and scarlet. The second layer was made of goat hair, the third of ram skins dyed red, and the outside covering of sea cow skins.

The tabernacle was to be 55 feet (16.5 meters) long, by 18 feet (5.4 meters) wide, by 18 feet (5.4 meters) high. It was to be divided into two apartments, which God called the holy place and the Most Holy Place. These two rooms were to be separated by a curtain of blue, purple, and scarlet, with figures of cherubim (a kind of angels) woven into it.

God asked for very little furniture. In the holy place, He wanted just a table for bread, an altar on which incense was to

164

be burned, and a seven-branched lampstand for light.

The bread—or bread of the Presence, as it was called—would remind the people that God would give them everything they needed. It pointed forward to Jesus, the Bread of Life. The sweet-smelling incense would tell them that their prayers, mingled with the fragrance of Jesus' love, would always be heard by God. And the light of the lampstand would remind them that Jesus, the Light of the world, would always be with them, lighting their way.

Inside the Most Holy Place Moses was to put a beautiful box, or ark, made of acacia wood covered with gold leaf. It was to hold the two slabs of stone bearing the Ten Commandments. On top of the box Moses was to put a special cover made of solid gold, a "mercy seat," as it is called in the King James Version. Two golden cherubim would gaze down reverently on it. This was where God Himself would appear in a holy light.

When you stop to think of it, it was wonderful for God to put a mercy seat between Himself and His law. He wanted His people to know that though they might break His law, He would always be ready to forgive them. They just needed to say that they were sorry and to ask for His mercy.

Then God told Moses about the services that were to be carried on in the tabernacle. He explained how animals were to

165

be offered as sacrifices. God didn't like to see animals suffer and die, but He wanted the Israelites to learn how terrible sin is and that death is the penalty.

Sinners had to learn that they deserved to die for their sin. But instead of dying themselves, they could bring an innocent animal—often a lamb—to the tabernacle and kill it. In this animal they could see Jesus who would die on Calvary. He is "the Lamb of God, who takes away the sin of the world." *

Day after day, for 40 days and 40 nights, God told Moses what He wanted him to do. God even named the people He wanted to be His priests. He described the beautiful clothing they should wear. Then, on the last day, God gave Moses a wonderful present. "When the Lord finished speaking to Moses on Mount Sinai, he gave him the two tablets of the Testimony, the tablets of stone inscribed by the finger of God."

What a treasure! Imagine what those "tablets of stone" would be worth today! Billions of dollars couldn't buy them. "The tablets were the work of God; the writing was the writing of God, engraved on the tablets."

Just before Moses turned to go back down the mountain, God gave him some bad news. "Your people, whom you brought up out of Egypt," "have been quick to turn away from what I commanded them." Moses was shocked. He didn't know what to say. God continued, "They have made themselves an idol cast in the shape of a calf. They have bowed down to it and sacrificed to it."

Now all the thrill of having spent six weeks alone with God was gone. The priceless tablets of God's law, which Moses held

167

← PAINTING BY HARRY ANDERSON

During the journey of the children of Israel through the wilderness, God called Moses to the top of Mount Sinai and gave him the Ten Commandments, written on tables of stone.

in his arms, no longer seemed such a treasure.

When Moses reached the spot where Joshua was waiting for him, Joshua said, "There is the sound of war in the camp."

Moses stopped and listened, then shook his head sadly. "It is not the sound of victory," he said, "it is not the sound of defeat; it is the sound of singing that I hear."

The two men hurried on together. Suddenly, as they turned a corner of the trail, they saw the golden calf in the middle of the camp. The children of Israel were dancing around it.

The sight was too much for Moses. "No!" I can hear him saying. "Not this! Not idolatry! Not in so short a time!"

But that's just what had happened. In less than six weeks after pledging to serve God forever, the people had broken the first and second commandments.

Terribly disappointed and fiercely angry, Moses hurled the precious slabs of stone to the ground. Smashed into a thousand pieces, they went clattering down the mountainside.

_____
* John 1:29.

Trouble in the Camp

(Exodus 32:20-29)

A S MOSES strode into the camp his face glowed from his talk with God on the mountaintop. And his eyes blazed with anger at sight of the golden calf. The people fell back from him in fear and awe. They knew they had done wrong.

Sheepishly Aaron came forward.

"What does this mean?" demanded Moses. "I left you in charge! What did these people do to you, to make you lead them into such terrible sin?"

Aaron hardly knew what to say. "Don't be too angry with me," he said. "You know how naturally bad these people are. They wanted me to make them gods to go in front of them. They said they didn't know what had happened to 'this fellow Moses who brought us up out of Egypt.' "

It was a lame excuse, and it shows how much weaker Aaron was than Moses. It shows also how little the people really understood God or His commandments, which, six weeks before, they had promised so faithfully to obey.

169

"What about the idol?" Moses asked. "Where did that come from?"

Aaron tried to explain. The people had brought gold to him he said, and then he added, "I threw it into the fire, and out came this calf!"

But an idol doesn't just pop out of a fire. Aaron knew better than that. God does not work a miracle to make an idol. Somebody has to make a mold and pour in the molten metal. This was no accident, but deliberate, shameful sin.

"Light a fire!" Moses demanded.

They did, and when it was hot Moses threw the golden calf into it. He let all the people see their poor, little make-believe god melting away. When the metal was cool, he called for hammers and set men to work beating it out into paper-thin sheets. The whole camp heard the noise, and everybody watched as the gold spread out more and more under the endless rain of blows.

Bang! Clang! Bang! Clang! Bang! Clang!

Hour after hour the pounding went on. Israel would not soon forget what God thought about idols!

When the gold had been hammered as thin as possible, Moses called for grinders, the stones that the Israelites used to grind their grain.

The people watched in amazement. "What's he going to do now?" they asked. "Grind gold?"

Just that. He broke up the paper-thin sheets into pieces and gave them to the men with the grindstones. "Now grind!" he commanded. "Grind!"

They went to work and crushed the gold into smaller and smaller fragments.

"How long shall we grind?"

"Grind on!" Moses answered.

So the men went on grinding until the gold of the golden calf had become nothing but the finest flakes.

The people might have expected that after the golden calf had been completely destroyed, Moses would just throw the dust away. But no! He had the grinders gather it up and put it into bowls. Then he strode toward the place where the stream of water poured from the rock at the base of Mount Sinai. The people followed, frightened and wondering.

They watched as Moses threw some of the gold dust into the water. Then more and more. "Drink it!" commanded Moses. "Everybody drink it!"

171

So the people came and drank the water mixed with the gold flakes that had once been the golden calf they had worshiped.

The time had come for a showdown. Things could not go on like this. The rebels might take over the camp and spoil everything God was trying to do for Israel. They must be punished severely.

Moses stood at the gate of the camp and shouted, "Whoever is for the Lord, come to me." It was an exciting moment. Would anybody answer? Was anybody on God's side?

There was a stirring in the camp. People came running—old men, young men. "We are!" they cried. "We're on the Lord's side!"

The first to come were the sons of Levi. Moses told them to take their swords and go through the camp from tent door to tent door, killing the rebels, not sparing even one.

It was a sad, sad hour. Three thousand people were killed. All of them had passed through the Red Sea and expected to go on to Canaan. Now they were dead. What a price they paid for worshiping that golden calf!

Face to Face With God

(Exodus 32:30-34:8)

THAT night fear and sadness hovered over the camp. The people had just buried their dead, and they were wondering what other punishment might happen to them because of their terrible sin in worshiping the golden calf.

They hadn't seen so much death since their last night in Egypt, and then it was the Egyptians who had suffered. Now 3,000 of their own people had been killed in one day—and who could tell how many more might have to die?

Moses was worried too. He knew that God was greatly displeased. In the morning Moses called the people together and said to them, "You have committed a terrible sin. But now I will again go up the mountain to the Lord; perhaps I can obtain forgiveness for your sin" (Good News Bible).

With a heavy heart Moses climbed Mount Sinai once more. As he entered the cloud and found himself in the presence of God, he cried out, "Oh, what a great sin these people have committed! They have made themselves gods of gold. But

now, please forgive their sin — but if not, then blot me out of the book you have written."

You can almost hear the sob in Moses' voice. That broken sentence, "please forgive their sin —" tells how deeply his heart was hurt. And when he said, "if not, then blot me out of the book," he was asking God to let him die instead of his people. Moses was offering himself as a sacrifice so they could live. Of course God would never have let Moses do that, but He must have been pleased with the devotion of His faithful servant.

"Whoever has sinned against me," said God, "I will blot out of my book."

For a moment Moses must have wondered whether God was going to kill all the people for what they had done. But in His great mercy God said, "Now go, lead the people to the place I spoke of, and my angel will go before you."

So Israel would have another opportunity.

God and Moses were so close to each other and understood

174

each other so well that they talked back and forth like dear friends. The Bible says, "The Lord would speak to Moses face to face, as a man speaks with his friend." This doesn't mean that Moses actually saw God's face. But Moses still longed to see God.

"Show me your glory," he prayed.

"I will cause all my goodness to pass in front of you, and I will proclaim my name, the Lord, in your presence," God replied. "But . . . you cannot see my face, for no one may see me and live."

Moses wanted to know where and how this would happen, and God replied, "When my glory passes by, I will put you in a cleft in the rock and cover you with my hand until I have passed by. Then I will remove my hand and you will see my back."

One day God said to him, "Be ready in the morning, and then come up on Mount Sinai. Present yourself to me there on top of the mountain." God told Moses to bring with him two tablets of stone just like those he had broken, and God would write His law on them.

Early the next morning Moses, carrying the two tablets of stone, climbed the mountain once more. As he stood in the crevice of the rock, he felt God nearer than ever. "Then the Lord came down in the cloud and stood there with him and proclaimed his name, the Lord."

The Lord passed in front of Moses, covering Moses with His hand. Moses heard a glorious voice saying, "The Lord, the Lord, the compassionate and gracious God, slow to anger, abounding in love and faithfulness, maintaining love to thousands, and forgiving wickedness, rebellion and sin. Yet he does not leave the guilty unpunished; he punishes the children and their children for the sin of the fathers to the third and fourth generation."

Greatly moved, Moses did not try to see God as he had planned or even to get a glimpse of Him. Instead, he "bowed to the ground at once and worshiped."

Like Moses, many boys and girls—and adults, too—would like to see God's face. And it is good that we want to see Him. But we can't, not yet. Someday we will see His face, but not now. We don't need to see it. It is enough to know that He is merciful, kind, forgiving, and "abounding in love and faithfulness."

As the apostle John once said, "God is love." * And because He is love, we can trust Him fully even though we cannot actually see Him with our eyes. But we can feel Him very close to us as if He were face-to-face, His face against ours, and we can talk together like dearest friends.

———
*1 John 4:16.

Called by Name

(Exodus 34:29-35:35)

WHEN Moses came down from Mount Sinai this time, after spending yet another 40 days and 40 nights with God, his face shone with a strange and wonderful light. It was so bright that even his own brother Aaron felt afraid to come near him. So were the rest of the people. Before Moses could talk with them, he had to cover his face with a veil. Maybe if we lived close to God as long as Moses did, our faces would shine too!

Things were different in the camp now. There was no golden calf this time. The people had learned their lesson. They were ready now to build the sanctuary that God had told Moses about some weeks before. But first Moses gave them a test to see how much they really cared for God.

Moses asked them to bring to God an offering of gold, silver, bronze, jewels, spices, oil, fine linen, and skins of various kinds. He knew that the people had all these things and that they had taken most of them from the Egyptians during their last night in slavery.

He could have reminded them that they wouldn't have had any of this wealth if God had not delivered them and that it all really belonged to Him. But he didn't. Instead, he told them that God wanted gifts only from people who were willing to give. If some of them didn't feel like giving, that was all right with God. They could keep their things.

"Everyone who is willing is to bring to the Lord an offering of gold, silver and bronze," he said. No one else.

As the Israelites went back to their tents the faithful old leader must have wondered what they would do. Up to now God had given them everything they had. This was the first time they had ever been asked to give anything to Him. What would they do?

Moses must have watched their faces. Some looked pleased that they could do something to say thank You to God for all His goodness to them. Others looked glum, telling themselves that if they gave up their valuables now, they would never get any more—not in this desert.

All the people went to their tents. Soon, in little groups,

they began to return to where Moses stood waiting for them.

I don't know who got back to him first, but it could have been a little boy bringing some precious trinket that an Egyptian had given him. Or it might have been a little girl with a silver bracelet she treasured very much. Boys and girls run so much faster than older people that they *could* have been first, couldn't they? And how children do love to give what they can to God!

If some of the children did get there before the others, I'm sure Moses gave them a wonderful smile of thankfulness. There may have been tears in his eyes, too, at the thought that the children loved God best.

Then came the rest. Bringing whatever they felt they could spare, they streamed toward Moses from every part of the camp.

"And everyone who was willing and whose heart moved him came and brought an offering to the Lord. . . . All who were willing, men and women alike, came and brought gold jewelry of all kinds: brooches, earrings, rings and ornaments. . . . Everyone who had blue, purple or scarlet yarn or fine linen, or goat hair, ram skins dyed red or hides of sea cows brought them. Those presenting an offering of silver or bronze brought it as an offering to the Lord, and everyone who had acacia wood . . . brought it."

It seemed as though somehow, somewhere, the people found everything they needed to build God's tabernacle. That's what a willing spirit does.

It must have been a wonderful sight—all the people bring-

ing what they could, helping the best way they knew how. And they looked so happy about it. Giving to God made them feel good all over.

When all the gifts were in and piled up around Moses, he told them more about His plans for building the sanctuary.

First, he announced the name of the man who would be in charge of the work. "The Lord has chosen Bezalel son of Uri, the son of Hur, of the tribe of Judah."

If there was one surprised man in the camp at that moment, it must have been Bezalel. And he would have been even more surprised if he had known that God had actually mentioned him by name to Moses on the top of Mount Sinai.

Blushing, Bezalel came forward. He was a young craftsman, not used to anything like this. Certainly he had never expected any such honor. What could God need from *him*?

Then he learned something. He discovered how much God knew about him. Pointing to Bezalel, Moses said, "[The Lord] has filled him with the Spirit of God, with skill, ability and knowledge in all kinds of crafts—to make artistic designs for work in gold, silver and bronze, to cut and set stones, to

180

work in wood and to engage in all kinds of artistic craftsmanship. And he has given both him and Oholiab son of Ahisamach, of the tribe of Dan, the ability to teach others."

What a youth! He couldn't have been very old, for he was the grandson of Hur, who had held up Moses' hands in the battle with the Amalekites only a few weeks earlier. But he was filled with God's Spirit. He was wise. He was a skilled workman in both metal and wood, a jeweler and a wood carver. Most important of all, he could teach others how to do all these things.

Few people knew that there was anybody like this in the camp. But God knew that He needed a good man for a big job, and He said, "I want Bezalel." God called him by name, so there would be no mistake.

It just shows how much God knows about all of us. He knows what we can do, what kind of training we have had, what kind of spirit is in our hearts. And He knows our names.

What do you suppose He knows about you? Will He ever call you to do a big job for Him?

Building the Tabernacle

(Exodus 36:1-40:38)

FOR THE next three months the camp of Israel was like a beehive. Everybody was busy—and happy. Having lots to do made them forget their troubles.

Young Bezalel was right on the job, leading out in all the plans for building the tabernacle. Helping him was a group of other young people almost as skilled as he was, and they were all *volunteers*. They *wanted* to work on the tabernacle. No wonder they did such a beautiful job! When people truly love their work, there's no limit to what they can do.

Moses turned over to the workers the piles and piles of gifts that the people had brought to him, and the very first thing they had to do was to sort everything out. Things made of gold went into one bin, those made of silver into another, and pieces of bronze went into a third.

The many kinds of precious stones made a sorting job of its own. The goats' skins, the rams' skins, and the sea cows' skins all had to be separated into piles, and the linen, the spices, the dyes, and all the rest had to be organized. When thousands of people begin giving, no one knows what will turn up.

And once the people began to give, they didn't want to stop. Morning after morning, they lined up with more and more gifts, until the sorters didn't know what to do with everything.

"Tell them to stop!" they begged Moses. "We have far too much already!"

Moses came to see for himself. The report was true. So he sent messengers through the camp. They told the people not to bring anything more.

I wouldn't be surprised if some were disappointed. I can imagine some little boy saying, "Mamma, I was just going to give that silver ring I've been saving all this time, and now they don't want it!" and his mamma saying, "It's too late now, son. You should have given it before."

Or a little girl may have said, "Mamma, I had just about made up my mind to give my pretty necklace—you know, the

one with the emeralds in it."

Her mamma replied, "You should have made up your mind earlier. Now it's too late." It *was* too late, too late for anyone else to have a part in giving to God's sanctuary.

As soon as all the gifts were sorted, work began on the building. Some men cut the acacia wood into boards of the right size for the sides and ends of the sanctuary. Others melted down the various metals, made molds for the casting, and began to beat the gold into thin sheets.

Some of the women spun thread for the fine linen. Others spun goats' hair for one of the curtains. Still others prepared the dyes, careful to get exactly the right colors.

Bezalel gave special attention to the ark, which was to contain the Ten Commandments. Because the glory of God would appear above it, he made it as perfect as he could. Of all the work he had ever done in his life, this was his finest. Never had he joined pieces of wood so exactly. Never had he beaten

out gold so smoothly. There was not a crack or dent or rough spot anywhere.

What a thrill he must have felt as he worked on the mercy seat! Imagine a mere man making a mercy seat for the great God of heaven! I am sure that Bezalel polished and polished and polished that slab of solid gold until it shone like a mirror, without a mark or a scratch on it anywhere.

Above the mercy seat he put two golden cherubim, which, with great skill and many hours of work, he had beaten out of solid gold.

When everything was finished, he must have stood back and looked at the beautiful, shining box with honest pride. But still he wished that his poor hands might have made it better.

Then he worked on the golden altar of incense, the golden table for the bread of the Presence, and the golden seven-branched lampstand. He made each one with the same loving care, hoping that God would be pleased with them.

Day by day the work went on. Those who were not able to help crowded around to watch as each piece of the tabernacle gradually took shape. Back in their tents at night, the Israelites must have talked about what they had seen just as people today talk about a baseball game or other popular event.

They didn't have radios or TV's or newspapers to entertain them at night, and the building of the tabernacle was the only thing of much interest going on for hundreds of miles around. Perhaps the things they saw being crafted so carefully made them curious about why God wanted the tabernacle built the way He did. Maybe many went to Moses to ask him about the meaning of everything. This gave Moses an opportunity to tell the story of God's plan of salvation over and over again.

At last, just six months from the day the work was begun, Bezalel reported that everything was finished. The tabernacle,

186

the lovely golden furniture, and the altar of bronze were done. The long curtain that was to act as a sort of fence around everything, even the rich robes that Aaron and his sons were to wear, had all been made just as Moses had asked.

"Well done, Bezalel!" I am sure Moses said, for it was a wonderful thing the young man had accomplished out there in the desert, with not a single power tool to help him.

Then, just one year after Israel left Egypt, on the very morning of the first anniversary of their deliverance, "the tabernacle was set up."

What excitement! Everybody was there to see it happen—men, women, and children. Never before had such an enthusiastic audience gathered to see a building go up.

When the furniture was moved in, Moses himself made sure that everything was put in its right place. He was the one who placed the two tablets of the law in the ark and covered them with the mercy seat.

At last everything was in order. So far as Moses could see, everything had been done exactly according to the pattern God had showed him on the mountain. But would it please God? Was He satisfied?

Suddenly, as everyone stood watching and wondering, "the cloud covered the Tent of Meeting, and the glory of the Lord filled the tabernacle."

It must have been a tremendous sight. Everybody was thrilled! But the happiest person of all was Bezalel. He had tried so hard! He had done the best he knew how. Now God had been pleased to accept the work of his hands.

Blood on Their Toes

(Leviticus 8:1-24; Numbers 9:16)

A S IT grew dark that night, the whole tabernacle seemed to glow as if it were on fire. In the morning it was covered with a cloud. "That is how it continued to be; the cloud covered it, and at night it looked like fire."

It must have been very comforting when people in the camp felt sad or lonely in the middle of the night, to look toward the tabernacle and see that warm and friendly light. They knew God was with them. On the blackest night the desert was never quite dark.

During the next few weeks some exciting things happened. First came the big ceremony when Aaron and his sons were made priests of the sanctuary. Everyone was asked to come and watch this take place, for it was to be something very, very important.

A big crowd gathered around the tabernacle that day. I cannot imagine how all the thousands of people could have had a good view. Maybe some of them stood on the surrounding hillsides. But I'm sure the boys and girls got as close to the front as they could.

And what did they see?

First of all, they saw six people come to the door of the tabernacle. In the center was Moses. In front of him stood Aaron and his four sons, Nadab, Abihu, Eleazar, and Ithamar.

Whatever's going to happen? they all wondered.

Then they saw Moses dip his hands into the water and begin to wash the men. First Aaron, then Nadab, then Abihu, then Eleazar, and finally Ithamar.

"Why is he doing that?" the children asked their parents.

"They are going to serve God in the sanctuary," their parents told them, "so they must be clean and pure all over—outside and inside."

Then Moses dressed Aaron in the clothes that had been made for him. Even from a distance they looked very beautiful, for they were blue, purple, scarlet, and gold, just like the curtains of the sanctuary. Blue was to remind Aaron—and the people—of God's perfection, revealed in His law. Scarlet was the color of sin, and purple was the blending of the two in God's loving mercy.

Moses placed a lovely breastplate on Aaron's chest. Each of its 12 gems were engraved with the name of one of the tribes

of Israel, and the precious stones shone in the bright morning sunshine.

On Aaron's shoulders Moses placed two large onyx stones set in gold. Each stone was engraved with six names of the children of Israel. In this way Aaron was reminded that, as high priest, he must carry the burdens of the people both on his shoulders and on his heart—always.

When all these garments were in place, Moses put a turban on Aaron's head, which had a solid gold band in front of it. On the band was written "HOLY TO THE LORD."

The shimmering gold seemed to make the words flash out across the camp. No one, from the youngest to the oldest, could have had any doubt about what they meant. Aaron was to be a holy man, an example of goodness before all the people.

While all this was going on, Nadab, Abihu, Eleazar, and

BLOOD ON THEIR TOES

Ithamar had been watching what was happening to their father. At last, however, their turn came to be dressed. Going from one to the other of the young men, Moses put on each of them a tunic, a sash, and a headband. These were nothing like Aaron's, of course, but even so the Bible says they were "to give them dignity and honor."

After this, a bull was brought to where the group was standing, and Aaron and his sons all laid their hands on the head of the animal, perhaps as a mark of their confession of sin. Then Moses killed the bull and sprinkled its blood on the horns of the altar and "poured out the rest of the blood at the base of the altar."

A ram was brought next. Again Aaron and his sons laid their hands on the animal's head. Then the ram was killed, and its blood sprinkled on the altar.

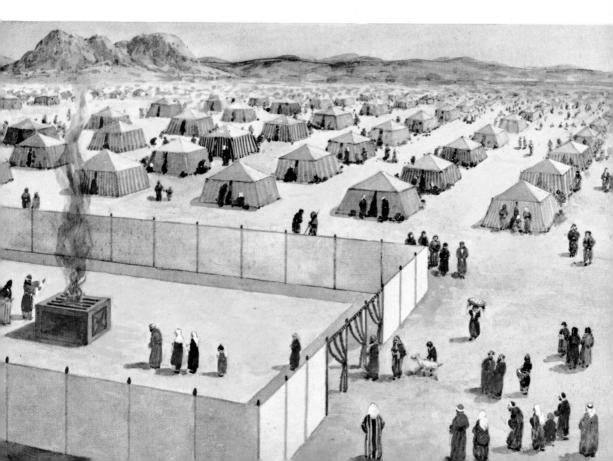

Another ram was brought, called "the ram for the ordination." For the third time the five men placed their hands in the same position, as though laying all their sins on the animal. But this time something different happened. In addition to sprinkling the ram's blood on the altar, Moses put some of it "on the lobe of Aaron's right ear, on the thumb of his right hand and on the big toe of his right foot."

Then he came to Aaron's four sons "and put some of the blood on the lobes of their right ears, on the thumbs of their right hands and on the big toes of their right feet."

The children looking on must have thought, *What a strange thing for Moses to do!*

But it wasn't really that strange. Blood on the ear meant that Aaron and his sons were not to listen to evil. They were to keep their thoughts pure, clean, and holy.

Blood on the thumb of the right hand meant that the priests were to use their hands for noble purposes. They were to be consecrated to doing good, helping the poor and needy.

Blood on their toes meant that they were to walk in the ways of righteousness. They were to follow the path of God's commandments, never wandering into places where God would not want them to go.

It all meant a complete consecration to God and to the holy work He wanted them to do. Today, as boys and girls who love God, we want to be consecrated like this too—hearing only what Jesus wants us to, doing only what He would do, and going wherever He wants us to go.